BRIDGE BUILDERS

Vincent Lassalle

Bridge Builders

Learning from those ushering the
future of society

About the author

Vincent is the founder and CEO of Adapt Innovation, a consultancy specialized in solution-agnostic innovation strategies. Prior to founding Adapt, he already had a decade-long international career spanning the entire innovation value chain; from research & development, to growth management, with experience in venture capital, change management and entrepreneurship.

He currently lives in Paris.

"Let's meet the time as it seeks us"
Cymbeline – **Shakespeare**

Back in June 2011, I remember the first of many unsettling work conversations that made me start thinking about societal transition.

A few months into my new job to help create the innovation team of EDF – the French power utility and the world's largest electricity producer. I learned at a watercooler that the main forecasting effort of this 160,000-employee multinational behemoth consisted of nine scenarios, only one of which allowed for the possibility for France to decrease (not end mind you, simply decrease) its nuclear generating capacity1. All eight other "possible futures" saw fission power maintained or increased, even though the world was still dealing with the aftermath of the Fukushima incident, in March of that year.

This essay is not about nuclear energy. Like any industrial process, nuclear power has advantages, drawbacks, and inherent risks. What was particularly disconcerting to me was that this objectively impressive company, harbouring some of the brightest minds I had ever met, and with huge resources at its disposal, was not considering any substantial changes in the next few decades that could affect its already unchanged sixty-year-old business model. Such stability seemed to me most suspicious.

Personally, I felt that many aspects of society were changing all around me : from the upheaval of entire industries by new digital platform models (Uber, Airbnb,

Spotify, Netflix, etc.); the global financial system in dire need of a redesign; a change in motivational drivers among some of my *Millennial* peers, focused more on purpose than de facto defunct notions of job security; to popular attitudes changing on societal issues such as Climate Change or Same Sex Marriage[1]. Nothing seemed so sure about the future to me.

Encouraged to do so by my hierarchy, I initially attributed this difference in perspective to my youth and lack of experience. At 25, what did I know of the world and in particular, the genuinely complex energy sector? Maybe every generation feels that their time in History is an important one. Maybe the feeling of the world changing around us is simply a projection of our inner turmoil and adaptation.

Over the next few years, however, I kept seeing more and more reasons to feel some deeper change was taking place. I gradually realised that since the world *is* constantly evolving, every generation is justified in thinking that their time is a pivotal one. Humans create transitions, not History. Maybe youth is just the time of life when one is more willing to contribute to that change, with enough experience for some measure of self-confidence and still enough naivety to feel that one can actually impact the world.

Today, old or young, most people seem to feel the world is living through some kind of transition : an acceleration of change in multiple sectors of society. From the more conservative perspective of a new Industrial Revolution (usually numbered the fourth of its kind) – around the digitalisation of the economy – to the more extreme post-carbon, post-ownership, post-work, post-capital,

---

1. 2011 saw the first polls in the United States showing a majority of people in favour of same-sex marriage.

post-truth... interpretations, many journalists, economists and sociologists seem to agree times are changing.

With our worldviews growing more discordant, in February 2016, I decided my time at EDF had run its course. I left the company in good terms, happy with the work accomplished there, and embarked on a self-designed[2] nine-month study aimed at better understanding this societal transition. If I wanted to contribute to this change, I felt I should understand it more than I did at that time. I had some theories but many more unanswered questions.

Aware of the litany of *post*-concepts, it seemed to me there was a feeling of departing an era, but not yet an understanding of where our voyage, our transition would take us. I was also noticing many new and old ideas whose time seemed to have come : such as Universal Basic Income, Direct Democracy, Localism, or even Minimalism. I decided my focus would be on "Post-Industrial Transition"[3] and to search for common values underpinning these various initiatives. My hypothesis was that if these values existed, they could be indicative of the society we aspire to.

I idealistically listed the questions I had about the world and the most ideal people I would like to meet to answer them, and began contacting them. People usually censor themselves getting in touch with renowned people, but in my experience, the more well-known the person, the

---

2. Surprisingly, at the time, I could not find any graduate or undergraduate program that taught current societal transition. Having in the past designed Learning Expeditions for executive committees of large corporations, I applied a similar methodology and designed a 9-month exploration of the questions I had. I describe the program more in depth further in the essay.

3. The term "Post-industrial" was coined by sociologist Daniel Bell in 1974, to describe a society where the service industry generates more wealth than manufacturing. The meaning I chose was the more literal sense of what comes after the Industrial Age. My premise was that developed nations at the very least, and the world more broadly, were in the midst of abandoning an industrial societal model mainly if not solely focused on production.

more generous and willing they are to interact with you. Once again, this rule held true and fascinating thinkers and practitioners ever so kindly accepted to meet with me. Here are some examples of the themes, questions and people you will read about in this essay.

In November 2015, the night of the Paris Attacks, I was sharing a bottle of wine with a friend, in a café just a couple of blocks away from the *Belle Équipe*, where 19 people were shot down. Lucky not to have been impacted directly by that night of violence, I still felt very safe in the world, but could see a mounting state of fear in Western Democracies and understandably, in countries such as Syria, much more impacted by terrorism. Was this fear justified? Was the world getting more dangerous? I decided to research the reality of the matter and also travel to Medellin, in Colombia – once the most dangerous city in the world [4] – and learn from its inhabitants how they overcame a permanent state of terror.

With the gradual automation of our economy and the foreseeable birth of Artificial Intelligence, I wondered if millions would be liberated from the current workforce to create new sectors of the economy – similarly to what happened during mechanisation in the 20th century – or would they, as some forecast, constitute the greatest increase in mass unemployment since the Great Depression. I sought out answers in Boston, from the MIT's *Initiative on the Digital Economy*. I also asked the opinion of Bob Collymore, the CEO of *Safaricom*, the most important company in East Africa, and Hitoshi Suzuki, *NEC*'s General Manager for Corporate Social Responsibility. Would the answer differ in Kenya and Japan, where every year, one economy gains nearly one

---

4. Even more so than Beirut at a time when the Lebanese capital was undergoing a very violent civil war.

million unemployed and the other sees one million people leave the workforce to retire?

Universal Basic Income is hailed by many as the social security model of the future, or is it, as others believe, an unfeasible, utopian dream that has yet again resurfaced since the idea was first introduced back in 1795? Free money from the government? It sounds a little too good to be true... or does it? Not knowing what to think, I ventured to Helsinki and met with the government and researchers who were to start trialling a version of the scheme in 2017.

Another idea whose time seems to have arrived is that of Direct Democracy. With issues of a global nature such as Climate Change and new communication and organisational tools, would the role of the citizen change in this century? I travelled to the birthplace of democracy in Greece, and met with Christos Karras, who works at *SynAthina*, Athens' online citizen platform, and on the other side of the world, Audrey Tang, a computer prodigy, digital Hacktivist and the new Digital Minister of Taiwan, weighed in on the question.

Society is also about beauty, art and our souls. I travelled to a factory floor in the suburbs of Beijing, where Alessandro Rolandi, an Italian artist is helping the corporate world and the art world to communicate and grow together. In London, Adam Parsons of *Share the World's Resources* (STWR) is working to create a movement to "awaken the heart" of society. And Camia Young, an American architect in Christchurch, is using the earthquake-damaged city as a laboratory for a new type of architecture and urbanism, one designed for human communities and not the transformation of goods.

Though focused on the First World – or as it is sometimes referred to, the Minority World – I still wanted to explore these themes in developing nations. I visited

Kibera, the world's second-largest slum in Nairobi, and met with Ruth Mwangi and Hital Muraj, two inspiring young Kenyan women working to develop their country through local economies and the teaching of technology skills to the most underprivileged among us.

Looking beyond our current issues and preparing minds to tackle the future is the heavy responsibility we ask of our teachers. I asked what children needed to learn from Leslie Medema in Bali, the principal of the *Green School*, one of the world's most progressive educational institutions, John Hunter in the United States, the creator of the brilliant World Peace Game, and Jonathan Dawson in Devon, the Director of the Economics of Transition Masters' Program at Schumacher College.

Overall, the study I designed took me to thirteen different countries where I met and interviewed some of the people working to build the future of society. This essay is a synthesis of what I learned from our discussions and how I now perceive our current era of transition.

However, to do any justice to the plethora of ideas contained in all these discussions, I feel I first need to give a certain amount of context to my findings. Thus, in the first half of this essay, I give a summarised history of the Industrial Revolution, and offer a brief overview of the current state of the world. I also give two systemic reasons that to me, justify the societal shift we must undertake, and illustrate a handful of reasons why such change feels so difficult.

This contextual section of the essay constitutes the intellectual underpinning framework for my study, and after briefly explaining its design, I devote the second half of this essay to the ideas generously shared with me during my travels. I explore some of the less discussed spectra of decisions our society needs to contend with today. Challengingly, my main realisation from this year is that we are fundamentally underprepared to address these decisions. However, borrowing from the people I have met along my journey, I share some of the solutions they have had to successfully adapt to this age of transition and shift to a post-industrial era.

Please, journey with me and meet the Bridge Builders, the men and women paving the path for the future of society.

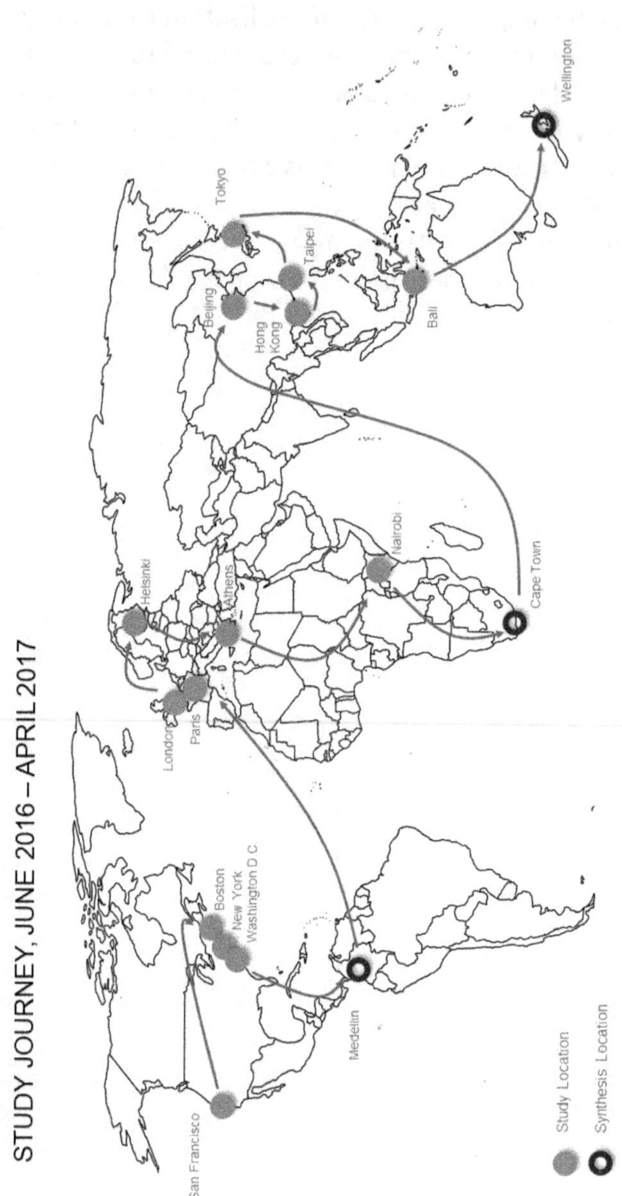

STUDY JOURNEY, JUNE 2016 – APRIL 2017
Tokyo
Taipei
Beijing
Hong Kong
Bali
Wellington
Helsinki
Athens
Nairobi
Cape Town
London
Paris
Boston
New York
Washington D.C.
San Francisco
Medellin
Study Location
Synthesis Location

1.

THE INDUSTRIAL ERA

Though no longer present in most text books, the term *Dark Ages* is still often used in the common vernacular to describe all or part of the nearly ten centuries of History book-ended by the Fall of Rome in 476 C.E., and the beginning of the Italian Renaissance, in the early 16th century. This sizeable chunk of time, constituting roughly a fifth of the "raw material" historians have to work with[1], usually brings to mind images of cold, darkness, illiteracy, alchemy, famine and pestilence, witches burned at the stake and people unlawfully subjected to all kinds of torture, ... in short, the bleakest scenes from Umberto Eco's *Name of the Rose*. However, this vivid depiction that endures in our zeitgeist still today, is at the very least incomplete, if not mostly false.

The term "Dark Ages" itself was coined in the 14th century by the Florentine humanist Petrarch, to describe what he considered a lack of quality in Latin literature during the Early Middle Ages and only over time, grew to become the more generally pejorative term we know today. Yet, starting with the weather, our perception of the times is wrong. The climate was warmer than previous and subsequent centuries. The *Dark Ages* coincide with what is known as the Medieval Warm Period, a time

---

1. Though there is no global consensus on this topic, History is commonly accepted to start at the discovery of writing, which we place roughly around 3200 B.C. in ancient Sumer, Mesopotamia, and stops 50 years before today's date. This arbitrary date is given to offer Historians a certain amount of "objectivity" on their findings. Thus, the subject of History covers roughly the 5 millennia from 3200 B.C. to 1967, at the time of writing this essay.

of relative increase in temperature which enabled farm animals to be more regularly fed on grain and not grass, and the thawing of the ice around the Arctic Circle, which Vikings took advantage of to take to the seas and colonise Greenland and other regions of Europe. Ironically and against popular perception, Europe was darker and colder during the Renaissance and the Enlightenment, because of the "Little Ice Age", than during the *Dark Ages*.

This "stunted" period in the development of human knowledge and science still somehow manage to see the creation of the first Universities and set up the basic principles of classical music. The Carolingian Renaissance in the 9th century, was a time of high innovation in literature, architecture and liturgical studies. It was common knowledge that the Earth was round. Autopsies were performed and the 9th century also saw the arrival of algebra and the decimal point system from the much more scientifically advanced Arabic world[2]. The hegemony of Western civilisation today unfortunately lets us often equate European History to Global History, but if the case for the existence of the European *Dark Ages* is questionable, it is a non-sequitur in the Arab World, which was living through the longest uninterrupted period of expansion and scientific discovery in Human history.

Monty Python in their hilarious *Quest for the Holy Grail,* were maybe a little generous with Medieval Europe's advances in public governance when they depicted an "anti-self-perpetuating-autocracy anarcho-syndicalist commune", but the feudal system did guarantee an increased level of security for peasants, Emperor Justinian's *Corpus Juris Civilis* (Body of Civil Law) generalised many legal best practices throughout Europe,

---

2. *The Compendious Book on Calculation by Completion and Balancing* written in 820 by Al-Khwārismī, is considered as the basis for Al-gebra and the author's name gave us our much-used Al-gorithms.

merchants were covered by *Lex Mercatoria* (Merchant Law) in their international trade, and Early Germanic Law allowed individuals to be tried by their own people, so as to protect them from cultural bias.

The somewhat enlightened *Dark Ages* show us that objective historical truth is somewhat of a myth. By no means does this authorise relativity of historical fact : the Rosetta stone was definitively carved before the invention of the combustion engine. However, the subjective interpretation of our past is the best we can do and all we really need, it turns out. History is there to help us navigate the present and our present discoveries in turn, allow us to constantly rewrite our past. As long as we do not counteract historical fact and our reading of History informs and helps our present understanding, I feel History has been respected and has served its purpose.

It is with this mindset that I wish to briefly explore the history of the *Industrial Revolution* and describe the perspective on which I built my analysis of our current era.

1.1. Pre-Industrial Society and the Revolution of Industry

In my previous jobs in Venture Capital and Corporate Innovation, I thought a lot about the nature of innovation and innovation management. I had to. Few panel discussions or interviews did *not* start by discussing what innovation was. My answer gradually became : everything and nothing constitutes an innovation. It is all in the eye of the beholder.

Innovation is much more about people's perceptions than the innovation itself. The difference between innovation management and normal project management I have discovered, is the added requirement to manage people's attitude to change. An innovation is a break from normalcy and how the rules are supposed to work. It is the perception that the chain of causality has been broken either in its expected direction or its expected increment. To some people, innovation is exciting and you must help them avoid making mistakes because of their enthusiasm. For others change is uncomfortable and you must help them make sense of the paradigm shift.

My view on societal transition is analogous. As I tried to show with my example on the *Dark Ages*, interpretation as much as deduction, governs our understanding of History. To me, the value of a historical interpretation is measured by its help in solving current issues. To study society's current changes, I wanted to explicit my own perception on the world's most recent societal transition – the *Industrial Revolution* – and use it as a basis on which to analyse present societal changes. So, here is my oversimplified narrative of one hundred and fifty years (give or take a fifty more on each side) of change-filled History in the West :

Pre-industrial or agrarian society can be most simply characterised by few in society having just "enough" and most simply trying to survive.

I am lucky that my father enjoys genealogy and so, thanks to him, I know quite a bit about my family's history[3]. Looking at the family tree one day, I was surprised that my ancestors gave the same name to several of their children. I thought they seriously lacked creativity, until I realised that each previous "Jean", "Marie" or "Pierre" had died, and this was sadly so common, that the next child of the same sex would simply take on the name of his or her deceased older sibling, this time hoping, he or

---

3. Nothing grand, I am in part the descendant of fishermen and lifeguards from the village of Biarritz in the South West of France on the Atlantic, and on my mother's side, descendant of mostly Irish and Scottish working classes, my maternal grandfather having left Scotland at a tender age for New Zealand, there not being enough work at the mine for him.

she would outlive the previous proprietor of the name.

The subsistence economy which preceded the Industrial Revolution kept the global population at around half a billion individuals for over a millennium. Rich or poor, if you lived in the 16th century, you would on average lose one child out of four at birth and another one before his or her tenth birthday. Epidemics of typhus, dysentery, influenza and plague regularly decimated populations. In just three years, between 1348 and 1351, a third of the European population died of the Black Plague (an estimated 25 million people out of a total population of 80 million). Even up to the late 18th century, 70% to 80% of household income went to buying food and any other purchases, including clothes and furniture, were considered luxuries[4]. Many children started helping out their parents by working at the age of four. Only one individual out of ten knew how to read up to the mid-18th century[5]. From Maslow's hierarchy of needs' perspective, the bottom level of the pyramid[6] – physiological needs – was simply not systematically addressed for most. **For such a society, "more" would mean better.**

Then after centuries of relative societal stability – through a series of technological, financial and social innovations[7] – manufacturing and agriculture changed, dramatically increasing the output and production of foods and goods of all kinds. With such success, even social services such as education became designed following industrial guidelines. If you look at our education system

---

4. All statistics in this paragraph unless otherwise stated : Carlo Maria Cipolla *The Economic History of World Population.* 1962

5. United Nations Educational, Scientific and Cultural Organization (UNESCO)

6. Abraham Maslow *A Theory of Human Motivation. Psychological Review* 1943

7. There exist many excellent books on this period of History. Not wanting to delve on the issue here, I can recommend two classics on the topic : *Industry and Empire : The Birth of the Industrial Revolution* by Eric Hobsbawm or *The Making of the English Working Class* by E. P. Thompson

still today, linear standardized classes with planned instances of quality control (exams) follow precisely the rules of factory design. This lead to a dramatic increase in the standard of living in all industrial nations : British real income doubled between 1830 and 1860[8]. Literacy rates in France increased to 96% in the same period[9]. In Germany, over the previous four centuries, the population only increased by 20%. In the 20th century alone, U.S. population in comparison, quadrupled[10]. The part of home income dedicated to food decreased to less than 25% in America by 1930[11]. Life expectancy in Japan nearly doubled from 34 to 61 years of age between 1820 and 1950[12]. Infant mortality dropped in industrial nations to 60‰ in 1950[13]. **By the end of the Second World War[14], the Industrial Revolution had successfully addressed the basic needs of most people in then, so-called Industrial Nations. If the point of the Industrial Revolution was to solve the lowest (even two lowest) levels of Maslow's Pyramid, then it did so by the middle of the 20th century, in under 6 generations!**

1.2 Creating Artificial Demand

At this point in History, this social and economic system – which relied on constant production growth and which had worked so well in the past century for industrial nations – was no longer driven by survival

---

8. Ideally, standard of living would mean « happiness » but the lack of data forces economic historians to liken standard of living with real income. Crafts, Nicholas F. R. *British Economic Growth During the Industrial Revolution.* 1985

9. United Nations Educational, Scientific and Cultural Organization (UNESCO)

10. Carlo Maria Cipolla *The Economic History of World Population.* 1962

11. United States Department of Agriculture

12. *The World Economy : A Millenial Perspective,* Angus Maddison, OECD 2001, UN Population Division

13. UN World Population Prospects, 2008

14. And post-reconstruction for Europe and Japan.

as the main reason for consumption and so other drivers were needed. To illustrate what I mean, here are three ways, generalised in the mid-20th century, to complement basic-needs-driven consumption in people : planned obsolescence, advertising and debt. One must imagine that to continuously justify growth these methods (and others) were added on top of a 14-fold increase in global population [15] and a roughly 19-fold increase in average global GDP per capita between 1800 and 2000 [16].

— **Planned obsolescence** [17] is a decision made in the design of a product to artificially limit its usefulness or functionability and to make it obsolete (either unfashionable of no longer functional) by a certain time. The practice originated in the American automobile industry in the 1920s, when car manufacturers reached a certain saturation in the market, but the term was coined and popularised in the 1950s. One of the most famous example is the 1924 "Phoebus" light-bulb cartel, where the largest light-bulb manufacturers agreed to reduce bulb lifespan to a standard 1000-hours. Rather uniquely it has to be said, the longest-lasting light bulb that predates this accord is the Centennial Light in California, a functioning lightbulb which has been shining light since 1901.

---

15. The global population grew from 500 million to over 7 billion in the last two centuries (UN World Population Prospects, 2008)

16. The world average GDP per capita was roughly $300 in 1800 and $6000 in 2000 (in 1990 International Dollars) J. Bradford DeLong *Estimating World GDP, One Million B.C. – Present*, 1998

17. Though *planned obsolescence* is usually cast in the negative light I describe, the practice can also be very useful in the democratisation of goods and services : washing machine manufacturers could probably build products with 50- or 100-year life spans but their cost would probably limit the number of consumers able to afford them. In turn, the economies of scales generated by a broader consumer base benefit all consumers in the end. A second positive aspect of *planned obsolescence* comes from a more frequent renewal of goods which enable faster sustainability increases : without some planned obsolescence, the renewal of cars for more fuel-efficient cars would be slower, and the overall environmental impact could be worse.

— Though **advertising** arguably dates back to Antiquity [18], the modern practice of mass marketing, designed to influence people's economic behaviour on a larger scale is a creation of the 1920s and again was popularised in the 1950s, this time by the advertising firms of Madison Avenue in New York : the now iconic *MadMen* of the eponymous television series. Using once again Maslow's Pyramid of Needs, the layer for basic needs having been addressed by industrial production, companies needed to create a new drive for consumers to justify production growth and they found it in the higher levels of the pyramid, in particular in "Esteem Needs".

— Personal **Debt** can be used as a tool to increase consumption. This is particularly the case in the United States or other countries using schemes such as Credit Scores. Credit scores are a measure of a person's creditworthiness based on the individual's past ability to reimburse debt. A good credit score will enable someone to borrow money at a better rate. One does not start out with a good score but achieves one over time. For this reason, it is important to have indebted oneself before one really needs to : to borrow for a car or higher education, or pay back credit cards, so as to achieve a good credit score when wanting to buy a really large expenditure, like a house for example. This encourages people to live beyond their means and thus to consume more.

1.3 The Gifts of Post-War Growth

Though not without serious issues – which I will delve into later on – this socio-economic system based on sustained production growth, continued global progress for several decades. Our headlines may remind us daily

---

18. Surprisingly modern political slogans such as : "*The late drinkers ask you to elect Marcus Cerrinius Vatia eadile. Florus ad Fructus wrote this.*" were found on walls in Pompeii.

that the world is falling apart, but if we take a step back, the times we live in would be the envy of most of, if not all our ancestors. Here are just some of the truly amazing developmental successes of the last half-century :

The world has never known such peaceful times. Unfortunately, often overshadowed by very real[19] headlines of terrorist attacks, refugee crises, or killings of unarmed black men in the United States, Steven Pinker's 2012 book, *The Better Angels of Our Nature : Why Violence Has Declined*, convincingly argues that we are living in the safest period in all of recorded History. The number of armed conflicts has declined by almost 40% since the end of the Cold War[20]. Furthermore, contemporary wars tend to be smaller in size and kill about 90% fewer people than in the 1950s[21]. Wars between nation-states – usually the deadliest conflicts humanity has known – have nearly disappeared. This in itself, is truly amazing. Homicides have also sharply declined. For Western Europe, which has the best and oldest available data[22], the numbers have plummeted for the last several centuries. Globally, United Nations statistics corroborate the trend. True, the number of deaths in terrorist attacks has been on the rise since 2011 – 78% of which are rarely mentioned and take place in just 5 countries : Iraq, Nigeria, Afghanistan, Pakistan and Syria. However, the global number of deaths by terrorism is lower than annual averages of the 1970s and 1980s[23], and represents a very small number of violent

---

19. As mentioned in the introduction, I was out at a wine bar, during the Paris Attacks on Friday, November 13th 2015. I am not trying to undermine the reality of these events simply that, as Bill Clinton said, to gain a more realistic perspective of the world, one should "*Follow the trend lines, not the headlines.*"

20. Uppsala Conflict Data Program

21. Micah Zenko and Michael A. Cohen : *Clear and Present Safety, Foreign Affairs*, March/April 2012 issue

22. Our World in Data, Max Roser & Manuel Eisner

23. *Global Terrorism Index 2015*, Institute for Economics and Peace

deaths worldwide (less than 3% in 2012 [24]). The world may not be a safe place and there are pockets of unspeakable violence, but as I witnessed travelling to fourteen different countries for this study, and more specifically, when struggling to locate Helsinki's one and only relatively small police station, it is getting safer [25].

Though never a linear process, **global tolerance, social rights and respect for diversity have overall increased**, in particular during the second half of the 21st century. Democracy may be "the worst form of government except for all others" [26] or maladjusted to our unreliable emotional nature as Plato argues in his *Republic*, but it does show society's recognition for the views of others. As the Polity IV [27] data shows, democracy has become over the last two hundred years the dominant form of government worldwide [28] and the majority of people on Earth now lives under democratic rule [29]. These

---

24. United Nations and Nation Center for Counterterrorism.

25. I also mentioned in the introduction having visited Medellín in Colombia, which in the 1990s, was the most dangerous city in the world. The case study of the former cocaine production capital of the world is fascinating and I would recommend you look into it. Sergio Fajardo, the former Governor of Antioquia (the region of Medellín) during the city's transformation, has given several talks which you can find online. Besides cracking down on crime, the two main factors which reduced insecurity, were education and connecting the poorer favelas to the city by building public transport infrastructure and beautiful libraries in the middle of the most dangerous neighbourhoods. I was personally surprised by the cleanliness and upkeep of the Metro system in an otherwise mostly bustling and dirty-ish city. Compared to most other cities I have been to in the world, the whole transport system was spotless, without any tags or sign of degradation, though it is used by millions every day. Once, I asked someone next to me waiting for the metro how that was. He looked at me bewildered and told me that the people of Medellín were very proud of their public transport. Even Bogotá, the country's capital did not have a metro system! Furthermore, they knew the role it had had in their lives and in the improvement for the city. He then put his hand on my arm, looked me in the eye, and told me slowly and almost softly that if someone threw a paper on the ground, the *Paisas* (inhabitants of Medellín) would make him or her "pick it up". I was even more careful to throw my trash into the proper bins after that.

26. Wiston Churchill, House of Commons, 11 November 1947

27. Polity IV contains coded annual information on the level of democracy for all independent states with greater than 500,000 total population and covers the years 1800–2013.

28. 103 countries out of 167 have a democracy score of 6 or higher

29. 58,6% of the world's population live in countries with a democracy score higher or equal to 6. Population data : The World Bank

numbers increased dramatically in the second part of the 20th century. Although the practice sadly continues in many regions of the globe, slavery is now abolished *de jure* in all countries of the world[30]. Starting with Venezuela abolishing capital punishment for all crimes in 1873, the number of abolitionist countries has increased five-fold since the 1970s and in total today, 140 countries have abolished the death penalty in law or practice[31]. Women's rights and LGBTQ Rights are much more complex issues where there are no simple indicators but all reports agree that globally the situation has improved in the last half-century.

Humanity has never been so well educated. In the last two hundred years, humanity completely flipped the figures of global literacy. From a *literacy* rate of about 12% in 1800, we have gone to a having a current global rate of *illiteracy* of just 17%[32], which every year decreases further. Half of the population on the planet learned how to read during the second half of the 20th century[33]. Nine children out of ten are now attending primary school and five out of six attend secondary school[34]. Furthermore, the difference between girls and boys is shrinking rapidly : from a 6% difference in attendance in 2000, it is down to 2% in 2013[35]. With, it is true, high discrepancies between regions, the world has never had so many university graduates : from only 10% of the global population enrolled in higher education in 1970 to over 30% today[36]. The

---

30. Though we may think of slavery as a legal battle of the 19th century, Mauritania only made slavery a crime in 2007.

31. Amnesty International : Death Sentences and Executions 2014 Report

32. UNESCO Institute for Statistics

33. OECD and UNESCO Institute for Statistics

34. UNESCO Institute for Statistics

35. UNESCO Institute for Statistics

36. UNESCO Institute for Statistics

internet is now accessible by 44% of the world [37] and mobile data is increasing those numbers rapidly. New information technologies are also democratising access to education across the world. Massively Open Online Courses (MOOCs) have grown exponentially since their creation eight years ago. Coursera, one the most used MOOC platforms, has known annual growth rates of over 2000%, a higher growth than Facebook memberships [38]. New payment schemes are also democratising learning in the Developing World. While in Nairobi, I interviewed Paul Mugambi, the CEO of *Kytabu*, an online platform which offers textbooks through a pay as you go digital format more adapted to the income patterns of underprivileged communities in Sub-Saharian Africa.

Humanity is healthier than ever. In the last half-century, the world gained on average 19 years of life expectancy at birth [39] and child mortality decreased by 12% [40], that is one out of every eight child living beyond his or her fifth birthday when before they would have died. This dramatic increase is due to many impressive developments. Since 1950, humanity has been able to drastically reduce many diseases [41] : Cases of polio have dropped by 99% from 1988 to 2015, Measles by 75% since 2000, Guinea Worm infections from 3'500'000 cases in 1986 to just 126 last year (a 99,996% reduction), Rubella has been declared eradicated from both American Continents in 2015, and the World Health Organisation plans to eradicate Elephantiasis by 2020. Though food distribution remains a global issue, farms worldwide currently produce enough calories to support a population of roughly 11

---

37. World Bank Data

38. *The Year of the MOOC*, the New York Times, NOV. 2, 2012

39. From 52 to 71 years of age, World Bank

40. From 18,5% in 1960 to 4,25% in 2015, Gapminder and World Bank

41. All following figures : World Health Organisation

billion people fed 2,000 calories per day [42], following a 200% increase of global calorie production since 1961 [43]. Since 1990, the world population having access to an improved water source [44] has increased by 15% to now 91% of the world's population [45]. The world's population having access to improved sanitation facilities in the same period has also risen by 15% to 67,5% in 2015 [46]. Every day, 250,000 people leave extreme poverty [47] and 300,000 gain access to electricity [48].

This historical perspective may seem abstract and incomplete – let's face it, I know and you know I am going to talk about the environment soon – but in a time of rather pessimistic headlines [49], it is important to realise how incredible our world is and how far along this system of exponential growth has brought us, and in such a short period of time. For the vast majority of our ancestors, being dropped in any part of today's world would be a radical improvement to the life they knew in their lifetime. This should not be understated, and to focus only on the challenges we face today is unjust to all the prior generations which toiled, innovated, sacrificed and fought for us to live this well. However, I believe there exists at

---

42. *Human Population Reaches 7 Billion–How Did This Happen and Can It Go On ?*, Scientific American, October 28, 2011

43. Food and Agricultural Organisation and World Bank population data

44. An "improved" drinking-water source is one that, by the nature of its construction and when properly used, adequately protects the source from outside contamination, particularly faecal matter. WHO/UNICEF Joint Monitoring Programme (JMP) for Water Supply and Sanitation

45. WHO/UNICEF Joint Monitoring Programme (JMP) for Water Supply and Sanitation

46. WHO/UNICEF Joint Monitoring Programme (JMP) for Water Supply and Sanitation

47. As defined in the United Nations Declaration of Copenhagen in 1995 : *"**absolute poverty** is a condition characterized by severe deprivation of basic human needs, including food, safe drinking water, sanitation facilities, health, shelter, education and information. It depends not only on income but also on access to social services".* UN Statistics

48. World Bank data

49. In 2013, a Outbrain study showed that the average click-through rate on headlines with negative superlatives was 63% higher than that of their positive counterparts. There may or may not be more bad news out there but we definitely look at it more.

least two true systemic limitations to our societal model which justify us changing it : resource management and inequality.

2.

REASONS FOR SOCIETAL CHANGE

Because the Kakapo genuinely is one of my favourite animals in the world, and that I unreservedly recognise Douglas Adams' genius, I will quite blatantly paraphrase this introduction from his 1990 hilarious zoological travel journal, *Last Chance to See*[1], where he devotes a chapter to *New Zealand's Night Parrot*. This lovable bird's modern struggles somehow perfectly illustrate the main issue humanity faces with its own growth today.

The Kakapo is a rather gorgeous fluffy, flightless green parrot from New Zealand. And before Europeans landed there – accompanied by a bestiary of continental creatures such as rats and stoats – the Kakapo enjoyed the privilege of being at the top of a very short local food chain, having no predator to persecute it. Like many species living in resource-limited environments such as islands, the Kakapo learned to limit its own numbers. The way the parrot did that was to create over time, one of nature's least effective and most complex courtships rituals.

In contrast, if you take rats for example, they are predated by so many different other animals that the only way for their species to survive is to multiply faster than they get eaten : the ultimate rat race if you will. For a creature without predators – such as the Kakapo – if they

---

1. If you have not read *Last Chance to See*, do yourself a favour, pick up a copy and revel in the depth of knowledge Nature gives us thanks to Douglas Adams' hilarious penmanship and observations. You can start by laughing out loud reading his chapter on the Kakapo, *New Zealand's Night Parrot*.

did not self-regulate then their numbers would increase dramatically past the point where their environment could sustain them. After the initial growth in population, there would not be enough food for all, so their numbers would dwindle. With fewer Kakapo, resources (food) would increase again and the number of parrots would as well. What biological research shows is that if you plot the number of animals following this pattern over time, the amplitude of the wave-shaped function increases. Each high in the population is greater than the previous one and each low is lower than the previous population minimum as well, until one day the population reaches zero and... well, that is that. So, the Kakapo learned to self-regulate [2].

For us humans, the story is more complex because we have learned to adapt the environment to our needs, importing food and resources from other regions of the globe, storing water for times of drought, fighting the bitter cold of winter with fire and carbon-rich materials. Thus, from a position very much in the middle of the food chain where growth in numbers was the only guarantee for the species' survival, we climbed our way to the top, refusing the fatalistic hand Nature dealt us. So, after over a hundred millennia of multiplying to save our species from extinction, in just the last fifty years, we learned that we actually were an island species. Our island is a minuscule pale blue dot in the middle of the dark ocean of space and we must learn to act accordingly, again for the species' survival.

We based our society and organisational systems on our old place in Nature. This has led to two systemic issues we must address today : growth and inequality. The first is required for the survival of the species, the second for its success.

---

2. Technically, the species was selected for its self-regulating ability.

2.1 The Limits of Growth

A phone call from his children's school changes the location of our interview from Bernard Control's factory floor in East Beijing, to Alessandro's car. The children are fine, but a slight misunderstanding in parenting schedules requires him to go and pick them up in the middle of our already four-hour-long conversation on art, corporations and society. Most people at this point would have simply asked to stop the interview. Not Alessandro. Good conversation can be had everywhere as he tells me. [3]

Surprisingly, Alessandro is an artist *and* a Department Head at Bernard Controls, a hard-core engineering world leader in industrial electric valve actuators. His Social Sensibility Department was created to improve social interactions within the company by actively blurring the lines between the art and corporate worlds. While listening to Alessandro discuss the importance of aesthetics in our society, I am struck by the scenery flashing by my car window.

Well, it is no longer flashing by, because we have hit some traffic. We are sitting still in a sea of cars, heading North, on an aerial section of one of Beijing's six four-lane motorway rings. To my left, the view towards the distant Forbidden City, is hidden behind the four giant cooling towers of the Huaneng Thermal Power Station, roughly one hundred meters away. To my right, as far as the eye can see, are twenty-story identical apartment buildings, planted every thirty meters like giant concrete hedges. I admit my description is a little misleading, since my gaze that day, could only reach about 300 meters in any direction. The cold and still weather of this brisk November

---

3. I do say middle of the conversation, because with his typical Italian generosity and appreciation for debate, Alessandro will then invite me for dinner that evening at his home. That morning we had never met.

day increased the Air Pollution Index to over 460 ppb[4]. My throat scratches. There are no shops, not restaurants, no trees at the bottom of these buildings. The fog acts as a colourless vale, which drains the hues from my surroundings. All is grey or slightly blue. This is also what development looks like. Alessandro is right, aesthetics is important.

At that moment, I wonder if this reality is just Humanity's growing pains – like the London smog was in 19th century – or is the illustration of a deeper issue we desperately need to address. After transitioning into the Industrial Age to drastically improve the Human condition, are we now forced to transition again to avoid our self-designed and self-inflected demise? Will the change in consciousness the Alessandros of this world inspire be enough to surpass the issues we have created for ourselves?

2.1.1 A few basics about growth

The true issue we face with growth is, of course, the issue of resource management. Not surprisingly our economic growth is highly correlated to resource consumption. This issue is that on one hand, our current systems in some ways, encourages infinite exponential growth, and on the other, we live on this very beautiful, very rich, very fertile and *very physically limited* rock hurtling across the vacuum of space.

First of all, exponential growth is responsible for the amazing increase in global quality of life I described earlier, which the first reason why our civilisation requires it so.

Our exponential economic growth comes mainly from our exponential increase in population. It took 123 years

---

4. Above 300, it is considered hazardous for one's health.

for Humanity to double from one billion individuals to two billion, 47 years to double again to four billion, and it is projected to double again by 2024[5], to eight billion individuals. Secondly, economic growth is also due to our growing individual's needs, or wants. Part of these needs are motivated by survival (more people eat more food, drink more water, need more shelter, etc.) and also by demand for ever-increasing comfort. This continuous increase in demand has become one of the cornerstones of our societal systems, which now encourages it, as I mentioned previously when mentioning the artificial mechanics put in place to continue driving growth : planned obsolescence, advertising and debt. I would like to digress an instant and describe the importance of debt and why it makes it more difficult for us to transition out of a continuous exponential growth cycle

When Central Banks abandoned the Gold Standard in 1971, money started to be generated by debt creation. The vast majority of the money in the world today – between 91% and 97% – has been generated through loans taken from banks and the future interests paid to them. There are many articles and videos online explaining this system, and I encourage you to look into it, if you are not familiar with how money comes into existence. However, most of these explanations seem to have a problem with the fact that "money is created out of thin air by the banks". They also often seem to imply that in the past, "at least" our money was guaranteed by reserves of gold and silver, and that that was somehow better. I will not enter this debate here but I think this criticism is missing an important point : the bed rock of any monetary or financial system is trust. It is no more logical to base that trust on an arbitrary-chosen glinting metal than on trust

---

5. UN population data.

that the future will bring more riches and growth. As long as people trust the system, it works. The issue though, for the purpose of this essay, is that without growth, particularly exponential growth, our current monetary system no longer works. To stop exponential growth, is to abandon this whole system. This is a difficult prospect to envisage and one of these problems we prefer to deal with later. But his problem only increases over time, so the more we wait, the harder it is to address.

I have mentioned that the debt system requires *exponential* growth several times. I wish to explain why very briefly and why less growth is not necessarily such an easy solution to our financial system conundrum. First, what I mean by growth is a steady rate of fractional increase in Gross Planetary Product (GPP) each year. For example, 2% growth means that any given year during the studied period will have a GPPyear2=102% x GPPyear1. This type of growth over time is exponential. If sustained it fast becomes infinite. Some people might think that if we had slower growth – let's say *linear* growth – then part at least of our issues would be solved.

So, let's imagine that we fix today's 2% growth and make it linear. This means that every year, the economy increases by a fixed amount equal to 2% of our economy in the first year. It would take us 50 years to double the size of the economy (instead of just 36 years with an exponential growth of 2%). However, after 50 years, the fractional growth rate of the economy under linear growth is only 1%, and over times tend towards zero. This forces us to abandon the debt-based financial system of interest and loans. Our financial system needs exponential growth and to abandon that means abandoning our entire financial system. Not impossible but, it does explain some of the difficulties to wean ourselves off growth.

With change being difficult, it is important to question if we really do need to transform or not. Honestly, it is a fair question. Humans sometimes like scaring themselves for no good reason, as shown by our pessimistic media coverage of this pinnacle in Human civilisation. Unfortunately, the jury seems adamant on the consequences of our exponential growth.

2.1.2 The impacts of exponential growth

The main consequence is that Earth's ecosystems cannot handle the rapid resource consumption increase, even with our planet's amazing flexibility and adaptive capacities. Earth seems so huge that it is a difficult notion to apprehend. People have tried to come up with simple ideas to illustrate this reality, the most successful of which for me is the *Earth Overshoot Day*[6]. Earth Overshoot Day "marks the date when humanity's demand for ecological resources and services in a given year exceeds what Earth can regenerate in that year". Any resources consumed passed that date, uses a limited amount of past stored resources. The following graph shows the trend of Earth Overshoot Days since 1987.

---

6. Earth Overshoot Day is hosted and calculated by Global Footprint Network.

Earth Overshoot Day Calendar

In 2016, Earth Overshoot day was August 8th. This means that all resources used past that date (40% of the year) was taken from the Earth's stock, or from future generations depending on how you wish to look at it. The *Living Planet Report* also illustrates what we know about our impact on global processes : *biodiversity loss, change in land use, global freshwater use, the phosphorus cycle, the nitrogen cycle, stratospheric ozone depletion, ocean acidification, climate change, chemical pollution (not yet measured), and atmospheric aerosol loading (not yet measured).* Out of these ten processes, our impact has increased on all measured processes since 2009 and we have gone beyond the safe limits on three of them [7].

If some people still have trouble believing that just one species – little old us – can have such an effect on such a huge planet, I would like to mention that we are not by any means the first to do so. Meet Cyanobacteria,

---

7. Biodiversity loss, the nitrogen cycle and climate change.

or blue-green algae. This microorganism is responsible for the *Great Oxidation Event* of 2.8 billion years ago, basically, creating our 21%-oxygen-rich atmosphere and the living conditions of most life on Earth. Sure, it seems to have taken the critter about 400 million years for it to achieve this level of production and we seem to have achieved global environmental impact in just a few thousand years, but let's not be too boastful, they are puny simple microscopic creatures and we have huge brains that make us super smart! Maybe not smart enough to understand fully what we are doing, but smart enough to do it much faster. So, we are not only an island species, we are also part of the select few on our planet to have acted on its environmental systems enough to change them at a global scale. Unfortunately though, unlike the algae, we have consciousness which may ethically lead to pesky old responsibility for our actions. But philosophy and ethics are also human constructs, so it is really up to us to decide what to do about our guilt.

In short, our *systemic* exponential growth and the consequent added-pressure on the planet's resources is simply not sustainable. If we do not change our systems accordingly, humanity will quite probably change the Planet's environment to one where even our great adaptive capabilities will fail and our species will be selected to go extinct. However, there is some good news.

2.1.3 Hope of change ahead

The growth in population is stabilizing. As John Wilmoth, Director of the population division in the UN's department of economic and social affairs explains [8] :"*The number of births has peaked, or has levelled off globally.*

---

8. Carla Kweifio-Okai and Josh Holder, *Overpopulated or underdeveloped? The real story of population growth*, The Guardian, Tuesday 28 June 2016

Some countries still have increasing numbers of births but for the world as a whole, we're not adding people to the population through births. We're mostly adding to the population because people are living longer." Though estimations vary, it is projected that Humanity will peak at some point in the mid-21st century and then decrease.

Basic needs are being gradually addressed for all and past a certain point of development, more stuff does not make us happier. As I mentioned earlier, global growth is slowly eradicating extreme poverty – even though, some would say too slowly – and giving access to the most basic needs to all. Furthermore, according to research[9] done by Nobel laureates Daniel Kahneman and Angus Deaton, happiness and income are correlated, but only up to a certain point. The figure of $75,000 a year is often quoted but is not so important. The fact that past a certain point, more is not necessarily better truly is the important notion here. Past this tipping point, material prosperity has diminishing returns when it comes to happiness and well-being. Once basic needs are addressed, the community in which one lives and the quality of his or her relationships are the best predictor of well-being. Out of the two growth drivers linked to human consumption, one is on its way to being eradicated (basic needs) and the second (comfort) turns out not to make us any happier.

We are increasingly efficient in our consumption of global resources. According to the International Energy Agency (IEA)[10], global growth in 2015 was accompanied by an overall reduction in energy needs. The amount of energy required for each unit of GPP fell by 1.8%. However, this fact though good, should not lull us in a false sense of optimism. Efficiency is a bit like the pump

---

9. *High income improves evaluation of life but not emotional well-being,* Daniel Kahneman and Angus Deaton,Center for Health and Well-being, Princeton University, PNAS, August 4th 2010.
10. International Energy Agency : *Energy Efficiency Market Report 2016*

system was on the Titanic. They slowed down the water filling up the ship by a few minutes but the ship still sank. It is true that even our impressive gains in efficiency are no match for the growth due to population and demand increases. Many examples of this can be given, such as total oil consumption versus the strides in car and plane fuel efficiency, but my favourite in the digital age, is that paper consumption is at a *"record high level and it will continue to grow"*, according the American Trade Body of Forest Industries.

Humanity is finally realising that it is an island species and distant prospects of population decrease and a reduced drive in material demand, may be comforting, but the negative consequences of growth are being felt right now and are only getting worse. It seems unwise and honestly impossible to wait for these issues to solve themselves over time. The environmental impact of Humanity's recent growth of the last two centuries, is reason enough for us to undertake a new societal transition. We need to find the way to stay within the planet's resource renewal abilities. We can do this in three ways : our consumption patterns, efficiency, and our numbers (population growth) [11] .To start with our environment's limitations and not our human aspirations would be a pretty sizeable transition.

There is a second systemic by-product of our current societal system which we might as well address if we are changing because of the environment : inequality. Inequality is not so much an issue of survival for our species but a question of improved well-being.

---

11. Though this last path would feel to most like a major reduction of personal freedom.

2.2. Inequality

I am a tall bearded ginger and in some parts of the world, this constitutes enough exoticism for people to start up spontaneous conversations with me, which I admit I usually really enjoy. This also leads more rarely and hilariously, to selfie pictures with entire families, babies in my arms and a grandparent or two by my side. Surprisingly for such a large and cosmopolitan city, a few of these spontaneous occurrences took place while I was in Nairobi and one incident in particular will stick with me for a long time I suspect.

Crossing the rather large Kenyatta Avenue in the Kenyan capital's CBD, a middle-aged man walking next to me asked what I was doing in Kenya. He was very polite, articulate and seemed genuinely interested. I will call him John, though that was not his name. Neither of us seemingly in any hurry, we sat down on a bench and I told him about my study, which had brought me to Kenya to question the impacts of transition on developing nations. He was full of very insightful questions and was very generous in answering my questions about him, his life and his perspective on some topics. He proceeded in the most matter-of-fact way to briefly describe why he was in Nairobi. A school master in South Soudan, he had six months prior been forced to flee his home with his two daughters after the murder of his wife, and was now staying with a distant relative in a small shack in Kibera, the world's second-largest slum, home to an estimated one million people. He came into town today to see if he could get a job. He needed money to repair the corrugated iron roof which had fallen apart in the previous night's rain and keep his daughter's dry tonight. While telling me these things he might not have brought up, had I not ask, he remained unbelievably dignified, though under his brave face, his grief, in particular when talking about his wife, was discernible.

Some of you may think that this entire encounter was a scam. Maybe it was – though I genuinely did not think so at the time, and you should take my word for it, I was there – and most importantly it does not really matter. Even if this story was not John's, it most certainly is somebody else's in Kibera.

I did not recount this encounter to make you feel bad about how lucky you are, convey pathos, describe how noble John was faced with such adversity (which boggles my mind though), or to push you into action helping people like John – though, if you feel like doing so, please do. No, I simply think that it is important to realise first-hand how unequal lives still are in our world. There has been a lot of talk in the last few years about the rise in inequality in developed nations, in particular in the United States. So, what of it? Is inequality on the rise between the Super Rich and the already exceedingly lucky like me? How about between me and the Johns of the world? This is the second systemic issue, I wish to discuss, which I feel justifies us transitioning out of our societal industrial model.

2.2.1 Global Equality on the rise

I will start with the good news this time. **Global inequality appears to be decreasing**. In accordance with the picture I have painted up to now, growth has been a remarkable tool for overall wealth increase and also equality. As the following graph illustrates, from a relatively homogenous but poor global society in 1820, global wealth increased over the 19th and 20th centuries (as seen by the right-shifting of the graphs). However, humanity initially got richer at two very different unequal speeds, hence the two bumps on the 1970 graph below. One part of the global population (industrial nations) pulled away and attained an average normalized income around the $5,000 mark, whereas the rest of the world was spread around the $500 mark, only marginally increasing their income in the 150-year period. However, in the last few decades, you can see the rest of the world – mainly due to the development of Asia – joining the richest nations and creating somewhat of a global standard deviation around the $2000 mark. The world is both richer and overall more equal. Since 2000, this trend has continued with the emergence of a middle class in both China and India. Yet, some researchers, such as Branko Milanovic, a senior scholar with the Luxembourg Income Survey now at the City University of New York's Graduate Center, cautions us [12]that the picture may be slightly skewed by national data sets regularly underestimating the income of the top 1% and global tax havens concealing still more income.

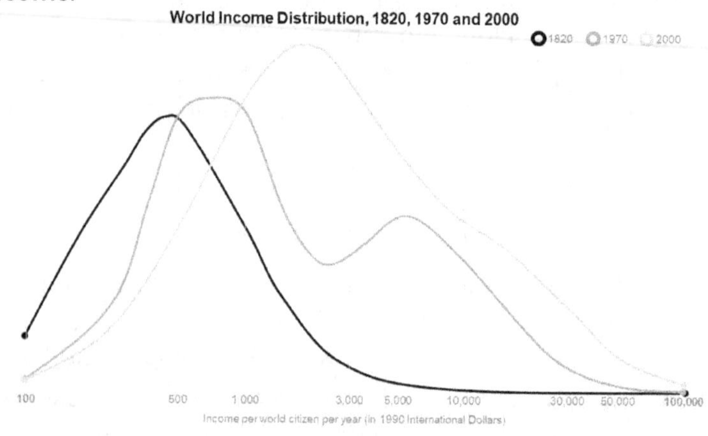

---

12. *Global Inequality : A New Approach for the Age of Globalization*, Branko Milanovic, 2016

Overall – with great discrepancies between regions of the globe – the world is gradually becoming a more equal and unified community in regards to income. However, the picture is quite different when looking at inequality within nations, in particular, in so-called developed nations, as an IMF report [13], quoting President Obama, stated in 2015 : *"Widening income inequality is the defining challenge of our time. In advanced economies, the gap between the rich and poor is at its highest level in decades."* Furthermore, wealth inequality is usually even greater than income inequality [14].

The factors responsible for the widening gap in rich nations, are complex and research is still being undertaken to better understand the reasons behind this trend, but the trend's empirical evidence is largely unchallenged. In particular, the increase in inequality in developed nations seems linked in large part to the strong increase in income growth of the top 1% [15]. As Oxfam published in January 2017, just eight white men – six of which American [16] – own as much wealth as the bottom half of Humanity. Because this essay's focus is not just on inequality, I will only focus on two systemic trends which contribute to the concentration of wealth among the Super Rich.

---

13. *Causes and Consequences of Income Inequality : A Global Perspective*, Era Dabla-Norris, Kalpana Kochhar, Nujin Suphaphiphat, Frantisek Ricka, Evridiki Tsounta, June 2015

14. *Causes and Consequences of Income Inequality : A Global Perspective*, Era Dabla-Norris, Kalpana Kochhar, Nujin Suphaphiphat, Frantisek Ricka, Evridiki Tsounta, June 2015

15. Krugman 2014 & *Causes and Consequences of Income Inequality : A Global Perspective*, Era Dabla-Norris, Kalpana Kochhar, Nujin Suphaphiphat, Frantisek Ricka, Evridiki Tsounta, June 2015

16. The world's 8 richest people are, in order of net worth :Bill Gates : America founder of Microsoft (net worth $75 billion)Amancio Ortega : Spanish founder of Inditex which owns the Zara fashion chain (net worth $67 billion)Warren Buffett : American CEO and largest shareholder in Berkshire Hathaway (net worth $60.8 billion)Carlos Slim Helu : Mexican owner of Grupo Carso (net worth : $50 billion)Jeff Bezos : American founder, chairman and chief executive of Amazon (net worth : $45.2 billion)Mark Zuckerberg : American chairman, chief executive officer, and co-founder of Facebook (net worth $44.6 billion)Larry Ellison : American co-founder and CEO of Oracle (net worth $43.6 billion)Michael Bloomberg : American founder, owner and CEO of Bloomberg LP (net worth : $40 billion)

Both mechanisms, should also continue in the future if no measures are taken to counteract them. The two processes in question are : the relative faster growth of capital returns to economic growth, and the impacts of a digitalised economy (winner-takes-all markets and superstars).

2.2.2. *The rich get richer and the poor get poorer*

The French Economist Thomas Piketty is in large part responsible for bringing the topic of inequality to the attention of many, in publishing his 2013 best-seller, *Capital in the Twenty-First Century.* It is difficult to summarise nearly one thousand pages of economic theory, but the main thesis of his work revolves around the idea that capital returns – what one receives by investing one's money – are always greater than economic growth. In other words, work always pays less than being rich and investing one's money. Bill Gates is a good example of this. Though he became the richest man in the world by creating Microsoft (work), he has made more money in the years since his retirement than all the years he worked at his company (investing). In general, this implies that inequality is structural.

Unsurprisingly, Piketty has attracted much criticism since the publication of his book, but most agree on the quality and thoroughness of his data analysis. Capital returns seem quite stable over time (around 5% growth), which would be a very high rate for sustained economic growth (other than in times of reconstruction or catch-up). The only time in history according to the French Economist when the capital return rate was lower than economic growth was during the post-Second World War era, when capital was highly taxed (up to 90% in the United States) and where economic growth was exceedingly high because of the reconstruction of Europe and Japan.

Furthermore, Piketty also shows that, in developed nations, the majority of wealth is inherited rather than earned. Yet, we live in a society that justifies inequality, on the basis of our living in a meritocracy, which is simply not the case if we inherit the bulk of our wealth rather than earning it. This meritocracy myth becomes increasingly hard to justify as inequality grows, leading to social and political instability and economic stagnation.

For all the reasons previously mentioned and chief among them national economies becoming closer to one another (the poorer countries catching up to developed nations), the global rate of growth is slowing down. Furthermore, because countries are competing to attract investments in order to increase their national growth, capital is being taxed less and less. The trend described by Piketty should continue to strengthen in the future. We are gradually returning to a pre-industrial situation, where a minority of very rich people enjoy most of the wealth, as the Oxfam statistic illustrates.

2.2.3. The Digitalisation of the Economy

This polarisation of wealth within developed nations is strengthened by the gradual digitalisation of our economies, as Andrew McAfee and Erik Brynjolfsson explain, in their 2014 best-seller, *The Second Machine Age – Work, Progress, and Prosperity in a Time of Brilliant Technologies*. These are known as Winner-takes-all markets. Take for example search engines, social media or online marketplaces, how many other companies can you name in those fields besides Google, Facebook and Amazon? Conversely, I am sure you could easily list ten car manufacturers or even pharmaceutical companies, both industries having known great concentration in recent decades. Furthermore, digital industries require relatively low amounts of human labour. Thus, the wealth generated by them goes to few people and mostly to the financiers who invested in them. It is no surprise that half the men on the Oxfam list are owners of such companies.

The increased transparency and consequent polarisation that digital ranking and filtering gives to companies is also true of people. Previously, compensation more closely tracked absolute performance, whereas today digital economies are mainly determined by relative performance. If you had a worker 90% as competent as another, it was more likely before that she would receive compensation 90% as high as the second. Today, digital filtering tools (think of Yelp-rated restaurants, Airbnb rankings, YouTuber channels, but also LinkedIn, TaskRabbit and all automated CV selection software) create disproportional returns – even in labour markets – for a few "Super Stars" and the rest have either what is left or need to find a niche, where they can become superstars themselves [17]. Winners-Take-All markets and Superstars are developing phenomena which increase polarisation of wealth and contribute to what Piketty describes.

For the two reasons previously cited – amongst others – inequality within developed nations is increasing, but why should we care? Inequality to some degree, is good for society, isn't it? It incentives people to work hard and take risks, which are useful for innovation and development, and generally seem to be more aligned with our human nature. So, why is inequality become such an issue of late?

---

17. Digital tools also offer the opportunity for global spread-out niches to be concentrated and addressed, making them economically viable, where previously they were not. The market for pink plastic life-sized unicorns is probably not big enough to justify making them in one country alone but if you can address all the people globally interested in such a product through www.lifesizedpinkunicorns.com (not a real site, sorry), then you have a business.

2.2.4. The problem of too unequal a society

Well, the main reason is that studies [18] show that above a Gini index [19] of around 0.3, the inhabitants of a given society are worse off across a whole range of social issues.

Before detailing what these issues are, I would like to dispel a common misconception. Some people argue that fighting income inequality stops growth. Actually, in rich and poor countries alike, research [20] shows inequality is strongly correlated with shorter spells of economic expansion, less growth over time and more frequent and more severe boom-and-bust cycles that make economies more volatile and vulnerable to a crisis. Income inequality is thought by many to have been one of the main factors in the 2008 financial crisis [21].

Moreover, as Harvard epidemiologists Richard Wilkinson and Kate Pickett show in *The Spirit Level : Why More Equal Societies Almost Always Do Better*, strong income inequality affects nearly every aspect of society negatively, including but not limited to : Life expectancy, math and literacy, infant mortality, homicides, imprisonment, teenage births, trust, obesity and mental illness (including drug dependency). The impact of income inequality is far from negligible, since problems in all these fields are in general from twice to 10 times more common in unequal OECD countries than

18. Kennedy, B., Kawachi, I., Glass, R. and Prothrow- Stith, D. (1998). Income distribution, socio-economic status and self-rated health in the United States : Multi-level analysis. British Medical Journal, 317, pp. 917–21

19. The **Gini coefficient** measures the inequality among values of a frequency distribution and is used generally to describe income distribution within a population. A Gini coefficient of zero expresses perfect equality, where everyone has the same income. A Gini coefficient of 1 expresses maximal inequality among values, where only one person has all the income, and all others have none.

20. Berg A, Ostry JD. *Inequality and Unsustainable Growth : Two Sides of the Same Coin ?:* International Monetary Fund, 2013.Stiglitz JE. The price of inequality : How today's divided society endangers our future : WW Norton & Company, 2012.

21. *Inequality and financialisation : A dangerous mix*, 18 December, 2014 New Economics Foundation

their more equal counterparts.

Maybe more surprising is the fact that these issues affect not only the poorest individuals of an unequal society but the rich as well. The biggest differences happen at the bottom of society for sure but even for the rich, it is better to be wealthy in a more equal country. Furthermore, in a world faced with truly global issues, research shows that more equal societies have stronger community life and that their people are more willing to act for the common good – they recycle more, spend more on foreign aid, score higher on the Global Peace Index [22], and business leaders in more equal countries rate international environmental agreements more highly [23].

Finally, income inequality erodes democracy. In a 2014 paper [24], economists Martin Gilens and Benjamin Page state *"that economic elites and organized groups representing business interests have substantial independent impacts on U.S. government policy, while average citizens and mass-based interest groups have little or no independent influence."* Though most often in the United States, the middle and upper classes agree on policy issues, when their opinions differ, the rich and business groups are more influential, though they represent a smaller part of the population. This in turn fuels the feeling of injustice that is at the heart of the whole matter.

As the British poet, John Donne famously noted : "No man is an island". Income inequality gives us what Wilkinson and Pickett refer to as "social evaluation anxiety". It is the fear of negative social judgement. It threatens our self-esteem and social status and it affects

---

22. Wilkinson RG, Pickett K. The Spirit Level : Why Equality is Better for Everyone. London : Penguin, 2010

23. Wilkinson RG, Pickett KE, De Vogli R. Equality, sustainability, and quality of life. BMJ 2010

24. *Testing Theories of American Politics : Elites, Interest Groups, and Average Citizens*, Martin Gilens and Benjamin I. Page, Cambridge University Press, 18 September 2014

all members of a given society, rich or poor, because it is an atmosphere that permeates all parts of society. Several studies show that tasks that raise our stress level the most [25] are those that have social evaluative threats. In short, we feel more stressed, less happy, more defensive and less trusting with high income inequality within our community. This in turns affects negatively all the societal aspects cited previously.

Finally, Wilkinson and Pickett's research interestingly shows that, though within a given society, income inequality can have wide-ranging negative impacts, there is no such correlation between countries themselves. This is because social evaluation anxiety only exists within one's own community and as of today, that community is usually found no higher than at a national level. However, historically, our community has always grown, from a few families in a cave, to a village, a valley, a city-state, a region, a nation state and today a union of states such as the European Union or the United States. Though not linearly over time, our social consciousness has gradually grown to encompass larger and larger groups. At some point in history (and we are getting quite close today), we can imagine that we will feel part of a global community of humans. If that is the case, the mechanics explained hereabove could operate at a planetary level. Without any research to confirm this supposition, I wonder if terrorism (global criminality), to use only one example, is not to some extent, the negative effects of global inequality taking place in our global community. If such is the case, we should really start addressing such issues by tackling global inequality, because as I mentioned, though inequality between nations is decreasing, inequality within nations is

---

25. Generate the most cortisol – the stress hormone – in the brain.

increasing. Taking the global perspective of our conception of community becoming planetary, this constitutes a much bigger issue. Just look at the (lack of) overlap between income spread between developed nations and Sub-Saharan Africa in the graph below, a regional cut out of the previous graph.

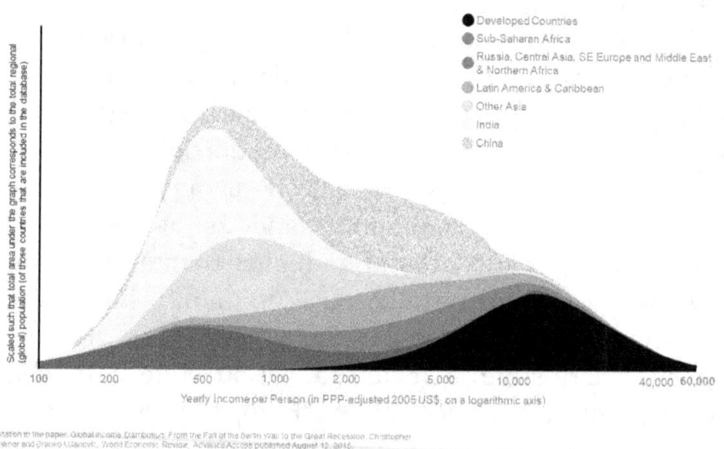

Our societal system is based on the notion of unimpeded growth. Unfortunately, the collateral effects of this are that this system has gradually become a threat to our species' survival. To prevent Humanity disappearing along with countless other species in the "Sixth Major Extinction" [26], we desperately need to alter our current societal structure and development processes. Furthermore, even if we somehow survived, this system also intrinsically promotes

---

26. Sadly, scientists believe human activity is responsible for our planet's sixth major extinction : the Holocene Extinction. A Major Extinction is when over 75% of species on Earth disappear during a geologically brief period of time. The present rate of extinction may be up to 140,000 species per year, which is 100 to 1000 times higher than the "normal" rate of extinction due to natural evolution. This is 10 to 100 times higher than any of the previous mass extinctions in the history of Earth. It is yet unclear if Homo Sapiens (us) will disappear but we are highly dependent on several animal and plant species and if they disappear, we will most likely shortly follow.

inequality and as described, this in turn erodes all people's well-being. Most would agree that a good society's purpose is guaranteeing and increasing the well-being of its members. **In short, our current societal model – though responsible for great progress in the past – is now leading to our ill-being and our extinction.** With such a dire assessment, why are some fighting to keep things the same and even defending this mortiferous system from changing?

3.
OUR STRUGGLE WITH CHANGE

Ironically perhaps, I have found that laziness favours action. If you take the various topics in this essay, I am trying to write as little as possible. I have given you, the reader, only three examples of how to "artificially" encourage consumption, not even talking about peer pressure and mob thinking. I have given you only two reasons for us to change our system, not mentioning moral imperatives of human decency, the value of other living creatures, etc. Laziness ironically helps me to act and action, as will become gradually more apparent, is the true point of this study and this essay.

For many years in my youth, I enjoyed imagining in great detail futures or projects. I can still remember the interior of five imaginary houses I conceived as a teenager, right down to the cutlery on the dinner table, the pillow cases on the beds and the light shades in the living rooms; house by house, floor by floor, room by room. I take great pleasure in day dreaming and "world building". What I have learned though, is that the pleasure I derive from "building" things in my mind satisfies me long enough, not to sometimes ever build them in real life. I now try to decide beforehand, which projects I simply want to dream about and which ones I wish to actually create. So, to actually act on something, I have embraced laziness, or a minimalistic approach to planning. If there is reason *enough* to do something, then that is good and I try to act. This is the logic I have adopted for this study and essay.

This essay is not about exhaustivity. It is not about painting as complete a picture of the world as I can. This essay is about describing the barebone rational which has made me think this study was useful to me, and has given me enough to start acting on these ideas. Exhaustivity, complete bibliographies, in-depth analysis of the whole situation, is impossible for such a large topic, so pursuing that objective is incompatible with the hope to act. The objective is to know enough to feel confident in taking a step forward.

With this in mind, I wish to look at *only* three reasons why, given that we know we must change, we still are so reluctant to do so and how we can maybe move beyond those limitations. These reasons are : our struggle with complexity, anachronistic sequentiality and the end of utopias.

3.1. A Misguided Attitude to Complexity

Usually, new solutions to existing problems are better – if not they are usually left to die on the paper where they were born, like a failed species in a Darwinian experiment – but tend to be more complex than the current solution to the same issue.

For example, though we may want the electric car to simply replace our petrol cars on a one-to-one basis and solve the environmental concern of combustion engines without changing anything else, it is unlikely this is what will happen. This change – like so many others – creates a more complex situation in two ways.

Firstly, the replacement solution only rarely fits the space of the existing solution. Electric cars do not behave exactly like combustion engine vehicles. Their means of refuelling is for example different. Recharging an electric car is closer to charging a smart phone. The autonomy of electric vehicles being lesser than their gas-guzzling counterparts, one tends to charge them at every opportunity when not driving them. At night for example. This means your home becomes your own service station and your car habits change. Not only do *you* have to change, the infrastructure in society needs to change as well. If many people start charging their cars at night – like they do their cell phones – society's energy consumption profile will change and so will the energy grid's production. It will of course, also affect the oil industry and their global markets and supply chains. This new solution comes with a whole new set of problems, or what we perceive as problems because these are new situations to solve or more precisely, new situations to get accustomed to. It requires effort to reconsider and wrap our minds around the new paradigm. This effort is one most of us have grown to accept for the benefits of progress but some of us do tend to resist it. The image of a grandparent deciding that they will do without a particular new piece of technology may spring to mind but this attitude can happen at any age and can depend more on people's personalities and risk averseness than the number of candles on a birthday cake. The electric car solution replaces a much larger and complex space than just the car itself. This is the first level of complexity due to a new solution.

Secondly and much more importantly, the new solution not only impacts the problem it is designed to solve – in our example GHG emissions by petrol cars – but usually also much larger issues. The change of attitude to the electric car brings us to question the entire and much greater issue of transportation. The electric car will unlikely replace on a one-to-one basis our existing cars because we realise that a better solution to the GHG emissions issue, is for the electric car to be merely one solution among a plethora of others. What will likely replace the individual car is a much more complex interconnected system of walking, biking, electric biking, public transport, car sharing, car renting and yes, individual electric cars. This means that all these different systems, managed by different stakeholders need to interact and redefine their areas of competence and responsibility. This change requires a great many stakeholders to change, some of which will lose out in the new paradigm if they do not adapt : in this case for example, oil companies. This is the real "cost" of complexity and what we resist. We all have to adapt and learn anew what we thought we knew.

We often focus on the effort added complexity requires us to make and we may complain about "how things were better/easier before", and yes, we all struggle in changing our ways. However, we forget that added complexity means that we understand more about the world we live in. It is a testament to our creativity, to our adaptive capabilities, to understanding our finer needs and our environment. A quarter millennia ago, our only energy source was burning wood. Sure, the complex mix of coal, water dams, wind, nuclear, solar PV, concentrated solar, demand response, storage, tidal power, decentralised generation... is a headache for power utilities, regulators, and us the client when understanding our bill. But, isn't it amazing that in just a couple of hundred years we have learned to harness so many natural forces and turn them to our benefit, that we are gradually learning to adapt to our environment by using the energy that exists locally and not forcing the environment to adapt to our needs?

Complexity does bring its share of headaches but I believe we should reframe our outlook and embrace it as the yardstick of progress our civilisation has attained. Solving such amazingly complex issues as Climate Change or redesigning our financial system to be in line with a responsible use of global resources, should less be seen for the effort it engenders but as an exciting challenge which could lead us to new heights. Complexity also forces us to consider more variables in planning before acting. This in turn, leads me to the second reason why we struggle to change : perfectionism.

3.2. The Anachronism of Sequentiality

Beyond the effort complexity requires us to make in changing our ways, it also gives us – today more than ever before – an excuse not to act. We are wisely taught to postpone action until we are better equipped to act and for many things that is the right thing to do, but for others, it prevents us from doing anything altogether.

If I take this study as an illustration, I struggled with one idea for three months preparing the study and one night, I found a solution and made up my mind. The problem I was struggling with, was defining the date on which to start the study, which could only be one year long for financial reasons. So much had been written on the topics I wanted to learn about, I could spend a full year before deciding on the people to interview. This would make the study richer without a doubt. Without preparation, I might pass for an idiot when meeting the experts I chose, not ask the right questions, worse, I may choose the wrong people to meet in the first place... I thought I should postpone quitting my job until I knew more. There was no rush and during this preparation time, I would still be earning a salary.

Had I done so, the choices of interviewees could have maybe been wiser, though honestly, I have met such amazingly interesting and generous people this year, I cannot imagine changing any of them. The overall quality, thoroughness and depth of the study you are reading would probably have been greater, but it is more likely you would never have read anything.

This issue of preparation before action, in a way of legitimacy, of being an expert or at the very least knowledgeable before doing anything really came into its own during the Industrial Revolution. In my native France, we say *"Quand on ne sait pas, on ne fait pas"*, *"When one doesn't know, one doesn't do"*. This makes sense in a world of increasing complexity, of already high complexity, but not too high. In this "Complexity Goldie Locks time" of the Industrial Revolution, you would not want just anyone to manage a steam engine in a factory. A novice Stationary Engine Driver, as they were called, could easily allow pressure to build which would lead to the factory blowing up. However, expertise for such a job – an engineering job at the time – was attainable relatively quickly and stayed somewhat stable for a century. Up to and including the 19th century, brilliant amateurs were the ones most often responsible for discovering what some call the "low-hanging fruits of science". Even the most erudite thinkers of their time, people such as Newton in England or Lavoisier in France, could contribute in one lifetime to many fields. Newton is best known for his contributions to mathematics and physics but his was also a philosopher, a theologian and surprisingly an alchemist. Antoine Lavoisier was firstly a chemist but also an economist and a philosopher.

However, the times have changed. In 1982, Buckminster Fuller remarked as much when he plotted his "Knowledge Doubling Curve". Up to the early 20th century, human knowledge would double approximately every century. By 1950, this same doubling only took 25 years. Today, on average human knowledge doubles every twelve months or so and according to IBM [1], the Internet of Things (IoT) could in just a few years from now, lead to a doubling every twelve hours. In such a situation, learning before doing is no longer an option for some topics.

Do not get me wrong, knowledge is still fundamental and I am in no way encouraging ignorance or justifying relativistic opinion over fact. However, we have to realise that expertise today is no longer binary – either you are an expert or not – but a continuous endeavour where one is in perpetual pursuit of knowledge. Even doctors who are given responsibility over life or death situations daily, who are trained for over a decade, would require an estimated 160 hours of weekly reading just to keep up to date in their sub-specialty [2]. For this reason, we must abandon the idea that action requires perfect theoretical mastery before attempt.

Thankfully, this idea is losing ground. The last few decades have seen the emergence of different methodologies of learning by doing. Open Innovation – the idea for corporations however large, rich and powerful, to look beyond their employee base to find new ideas, is a testament to the fact that problems today, have too many different moving parts for even the most resourceful organisations to fully comprehend and act upon internally. Design Thinking, Agile, Lean Start-up are all ways in the business world to "fail fast and fail forward", in other words to try in a way where mistakes are not a calamity but a learning tool to go onto the next step. However, many of us are still hindered by our deference to "those who know best", by the idea that "I am not the right person to... ", by invoking that "But I

---

1. *The toxic terabyte : How data-dumping threatens business efficiency*, IBM Global Technology Services July 2006

2. *The Second Machine Age – Work, Progress, and Prosperity in a Time of Brilliant Technologies*, Andrew McAfee and Erik Brynjolfsson, 2014

know nothing about...". We look to governments, large corporations, the United Nations, or experts to tell us what to do to combat climate change for instance, and too rarely still, take initiatives ourselves and invest time understanding and above all acting.

Another way this legitimacy issue arises is for people to be once removed from the actual problems. Few people seem to be directly addressing issues such as climate change compared to the number of social incubators, impact investing funds, and life coaches, all supposedly helping the problem-solvers to act. I do not want to minimize the importance of this type of work and it is great that an ecosystem for change-makers is gradually being built. I just feel that many people in these supporting roles are there because they feel, they should contribute to the change but do not think they can do so directly. I wish they would change their perspective and realise that we all can contribute directly to finding solutions.

Humanity has achieved a level of complexity that, as mentioned before, I feel should be celebrated but which also makes all of us once again responsible for acting. The era of delegating complex decisions to experts is behind us. Even the best experts cannot master and foresee all the variables anymore, and change is a shared responsibility we all carry. We must all be humble about our ignorance and invest time in understanding enough to be able to act, and act in a way that teaches us more information to act further. Like walking, change is a perpetual state of unbalance. Legitimacy to act no longer comes from a piece of paper or a title, but from action. Since we can no longer perfectly prepare, then we should embrace action as the way to prepare for more action.

Though I believe in acting more when faced with complex issues, I know that stepping into the unknown is difficult and oftentimes reckless. Creativity is Humanity's most wonderful tool to disperse the fogs of future mysteries, but sadly, I feel we have stopped using it as much as we should. Faced with the great unknown, we should call upon utopias to help us build momentum.

3.3. Our Need for Utopias

Amazingly but dangerously, we have successfully made utopias into realistic objectives. Unfortunately, that has made the future both lame and frightening. As Victor Hugo wrote *"Utopia is tomorrow's reality"* [3], which implies that without utopia, we have no future.

Rutger Bregman, in his 2016 book *Utopias for Realists : How we can build the ideal world*, argues that developed nations may have nearly achieved the utopias imagined by prior generations. Most humans Utopias can be boiled down to one of the most famous : The Land of Cockaigne. Cockaigne is a fictitious land imagined at the end of the Dark Ages [4], where there is no more sickness, where food and water are abundant and do not require toil. In Cockaigne, there are no wars and work is prohibited. Without repeating prior sections of this essay, we are close to achieving or have achieved such a reality in the Minority World. We live much longer than prior generations, mostly free of pain and disease. For over two generations, Western Europe has been at peace. Food is abundant and drinkable water flows from taps everywhere. If you are incapable of working, our social system will make sure that you do not starve and even have a roof above your head. For the most privileged, work is seen more as a path to personal

---

3. « L'utopie est la réalité de demain »

4. The exact origin is unclear but Massimo Montanari, Professor of Medieval studies at the University of Bologna, dates the apparition of such a land between the 12th and 14th centuries (*La fame e l'abbondanza : Storia dell'alimentazione in Europa*, 1993)

development than a means of survival. We even get several weeks of paid vacation a year, in most countries. To anyone in the 12th century, we live in Cockaigne.

We may feel that there is still a lot to be done, that there are still a lot of poor people, that equality between the sexes is not yet a reality, that some people work three jobs just to make ends meet. And all this is true. But one thing I learned during my master's in Project Management, is that for the last part of any project, one needs to *over*-allocate resources because with the feeling of completion nearing, people gradually stop working. This is what happens to the vast majority of us when moving into a house. We set up 90% of our things the way we want, but never get around to oiling that squeaky cupboard door or unpacking that final box of stuff we nearly ever use. So, even if there is still a lot to be done, the remaining issues feel somehow manageable, somehow like realistic goals and no longer like a utopia. It is only a matter of time before women and men have equal pay at the work place. Sure, it is frustrating that it has not yet happened or is not happening faster – like that cupboard squeaking every time you open it – but, it is no longer in our minds a question of if it happens, but when.

Achieving this slow pace of incremental improvement is another testament to Humanity's amazing progress. Our ancestors could only dream of a time when there was enough food for all. Even 70 years ago, the idea of a peaceful Europe was naïve. Fifty years ago, putting men on the Moon was an ambitious president's fantasy. Yet, today, we are working on fine tuning this reality. All our dreams seem achievable, or worse achieved. It is just a matter of time and resource allocation. Even going to Mars, or solving world hunger, sounds like something we could do, if only we really wanted to. We have run out of Utopias, we have run out of impossible dreams and are setting achievable goals.

Now, you may ask why utopias are important. Well as Buckminster Fuller said *"You never change things by fighting the existing reality. To change something, build a new model that makes the existing model obsolete."* At the moment, we are reacting to History, we are suffering through it. We react to climate change, we are not building a new paradigm. We are not building a new model, we are improving the existing one, even if it may already be obsolete.

The future is unknown and we fear the unknown. We have been selected to do so by nature. Our ancestors who were not afraid of the unknown rustling sounds in the grass, usually ended up swiftly dying before they could pass on their optimistic care-free genes. Utopias help us to make sense of the future, turn the fear of the unknown into the excitement of promise and dreams. Without utopias, without vision, without that excitement, we find reassurance somewhere else, or more precisely, sometime else. We find it in the past.

This is for me one of the main reasons for the recent rise in populism. Brexit in the United Kingdom, Trump in the United States, Le Pen in France, all aim to bring us back to the past. All wish to bring us back to a certain fictional vision of the late 1940s and 1950s. If you look at the *Front National*'s economic program for the 2017 French Presidential Elections, it resembled greatly that of the Resistance Government of 1946 : nationalisations of the industry, national preference, a strong Franc, etc. Trump wants to "Make America Great Again". All these movements are focused on the past.

The present is always messy and unintelligible. The rules governing it are unclear to us because we cannot foresee the outcomes. As I have mentioned before, this is the reason why historians wait half a century before analysing any event, to know some of the consequences of actions taken and describe causality. Without the understanding of consequence, we struggle to make decisions and postpone them as much as we can [5], or we make up imaginary conventions for how the rules operate. Either we forecast a future where the rules make sense : Christianity explains human suffering by the notions of heaven and hell. The Reagan administration justified tax breaks for the rich by invoking "trickle-down economics", which facts suggests does not work [6]. Or, we blame the rules changing on a minority group and try to return to a set of rules we understand. The group blamed is usually immigrants or a minority religion : European Jews in the 1930s for example, Eastern European immigrants in Britain and "Bad Mexican Hombres" in Trump's America. The set of rules we understand are necessarily in our past for us to make sense of them. Currently, the post Second World War era seems to be the golden age of choice.

Unfortunately, returning to past eras is as unlikely if not more so than reaching a future utopia. The reason for that is that we usually leave past eras for good reasons. Why did we leave the mythical 1950s? Because, that era of impressive economic growth required the reconstruction of Japan and Europe after the Second World War, and we are not ready I believe, to destroy a continent again simply to justify economic growth. The Cold War also allowed the investment in huge government projects. For Trump's America to be great again, it would most likely require the emergence of another superpower. In other words,

---

5. Evolution teaches us that the worse strategy is staying still and not adapting. Postponing change, though easier, is also more dangerous for the species on the long run.

6. *Reaganomics*, William A. Niskanen, Library of Economics and Liberty and *The Big Squeeze*, Steven Greenhouse, pp. 6-9

"America first" but another nation close behind, if not just in front. This 1950s-world some of us seem to long for also required the exploitation of colonies and the inequality in rights for many minorities. Most countries had not legalised the vote for women by 1950 and the Civil Rights era of the 1960s was yet to come. As shown previously, this world also required great inequalities among nations in the world. The worlds currently proposed by these populist movements are utopias as well, actually, they are uchronias : they never really existed and cannot exist within our time.

These visions do not exist anymore because we chose to address – and mostly solve – many issues from the late 1940s and 1950s to create a world where the dreams of Martin Luther King have mostly come true, where men landed on the Moon, where Monnet, Adenhauer, Spaak and Schuman built a peaceful Europe, where a wall was torn down in Berlin, where Gandhi would no longer need to go on a hunger strike to fight for India's independence, where billions have stopped dying of hunger and thirst. As I have said before, I believe we made the right choice to leave that era, and today we both cannot go back and we should not want to.

We are in dire need of Utopias to excite us about the future, to create momentum and to stop us returning to golden ages that only shine on the surface. A conflict diamond would be a more accurate description I feel. Yes, the future is complex but that is good and should be a source of pride. Yes, the future is unsure and frightening but it can also be exciting and full of possibilities. And yes, we need ambition and positivity, not a reaction to the situation but initiative, and innovation. That is how we can change. We need to reframe the fear and ignorance we feel into exhilaration and action, into narratives that make sense of the world, reduce the risk of stepping into the future, and give us hope. The only way is forward.

4.

DESIGNING THE STUDY

What you have read up to now summarises the historical perspective and the contextual outlook on the world, on which I based the design of my study. I felt it was important to give you the reader, the perspective with which I embarked on my study, so that we may journey together. The last piece of information I wish to give you before we meet those I have decided to name the *Bridge Builders*, is a very brief description of the methodology of my study. This will hopefully explain the choices of country along our trip and who we will meet there.

I created my own program out of necessity. Though initially I searched, I could not find a graduate or undergraduate degree anywhere in the world, which covered contemporary societal transition[1]. Not finding a recognised and accredited way of learning what I was interested in, I intuited that my case would become more and more common in the future and so, decided to undertake my own self-directed study. The pace of information generation being exponential and universities logically requiring time to gather knowledge and turn it into teachable syllabuses, I believe more and more topics will gradually find themselves outside the scope of teaching of even the best, most up-to-date institutions. What universities have and hopefully will retain, is

---

1. I finally did discover a Master's program in Economics of Transition at Schumacher College in England, but by that stage, I had done all the preparatory work for my own program so chose for better or worse to go forward with my creation instead.

pedagogy. With this insight, I was lucky to convince two supportive professors, Sebastien Descours at the Sorbonne and Vincent Dahirel at the Centre of Research and Interdisciplinarity, both in Paris, to take a chance on me and become supervisors for my experimental format. They would allow me to generate the content and help me with learning from my experiences.

The topic of contemporary global societal change being so large and, by definition, continuously evolving, I chose to use an inductive approach. I decided to concentrate on various initiatives in the last ten years in all areas of society. These initiatives were not necessarily new ideas but ideas which time seemed to have come. These ideas could be in socio-economic dynamics, for instance looking at automation and the digital economy, in public governance with ideas such as basic income or direct democracy, in the corporate world with non-hierarchical organisational structures or the increasing focus for purposeful careers, or at a more personal and individual level with for example, minimalism and localism. My idea was to try to understand the underlying values of each of these initiatives and see if there were any commonalities between them and across their manifestations in different cultures and countries. If there were, my supposition was that these values could be the ones global society was currently aspiring to generalise across our societal system [2].

Some may be surprised *not* to see in my list of topics such important issues as energy transition, our response to climate change, or even transhumanism. The reason for

---

[2]. Similar to Science Fiction or Fantasy, these common values would tell us more about our present than the future. These literary genres are ways for us to take a step back from our present and revaluate it through the prism of a different world. For these reasons, these common values, if they existed, would not describe the future. Nobody can accurately do that, but they may show us the future we think we want today.

this is that I consider these as reaction to a given situation or variations on existing values, so not as indicative of change as the other initiatives I mentioned. Our answer to Climate Change is a reaction to a current state of affairs, aimed to ensure the survival of our species, one of the most engrained values in all creatures on Earth. Transhumanism to me is the continuation of our quest for immortality, not by any means a recent idea. Just look at the pyramids in Egypt. Transhumanism will lead to important questions about what it means to be human. We will have to show initiative and define our society because of the research currently undertaken, but, for now, I do not consider it illustrative of new societal values.

Choosing locations where these initiatives were most developed, I visited over a dozen countries[3] over a seven-month period and was incredibly fortunate to meet with a wide range of absolutely fascinating experts, academics and practitioners, who generously shared their experiences and insights with me. The following table lists those whose transcribed interviews you can find the study's website[4], but there were many more friends and strangers along the way – too many to name – who also selflessly shared their perspective with me. All have contributed to this study and I am of course, enormously indebted and grateful to all of them.

---

3. See map on page 1.

4. http ://www.whathappensnow.xyz/discussions

Bridge Builders

NAME	POSITION	LOCATION
Michel BAUWENS	Economist (Economics of Commons)	Thailand
CHAN Kin-Man	Co-Instigator of Occupy Central with Love and Peace	Hong Kong
Bob COLLYMORE	CEO of *Safaricom*	Kenya
Stéphane CORCUFF	Researcher at the French Centre for Research on Contemporary China	Taiwan
Jonathan DAWSON	Professor of Economics at Schumacher College	United Kingdom
Jason HSU	Member of Parliament	Taiwan
John HUNTER	Teacher and creator of the World Peace Game	U.S.A.
Olli KANGAS & Ville-Veikko PULKKA	Respectively Head of Research and Researcher at Kela	Finland
Christos KARRAS	Communications Manager at *SynAthina*	Greece
Gaspard KOENIG	Professor of Philosophy and Founder of *Génération Libre*	France
Emily LAU	Chairperson of the Democratic Party	Hong Kong
Leslie MEDEMA	Head of Academics (Principal) and Head of Primary School at the *Green School*	Indonesia

Bridge Builders

NAME	POSITION	LOCATION
Roope MOKKA	Founder of *DemosHelsinki*	Finland
Paul MUGAMBI	CEO of *Kytabu*	Kenya
Hital MURAJ	Manager of Corporate Affairs at *Cisco* Kenya	Kenya
Ruth MWANGI	Director at *Grassroots Economics*	Kenya
Adam PARSONS	Share the World's Resources	United Kingdom
Alessandro ROLANDI	Social Sensibility Manager at *Bernard Controls*	China
Hitoshi SUZUKI	CSR General Manager at *NEC*	Japan
Audrey TANG	Digital Minister	Taiwan
Tanji TANIMOTO	Professor of Business and Society at Waseda University	Japan
Timo A. TANNINEN	Ministerial Counsellor for Finance at the Finnish Ministry of Social Affairs and Health	Finland
Joshua VIAL	Instigator at *Enspiral*	New Zealand
Camia YOUNG	Architect and Founder of *OHU*	New Zealand

I decided to transcribe the entirety of these discussions so that you may find other teachings than the ones I will focus on in the following sections of this essay. They are bursting with many fascinating ideas and concepts and I strongly encourage you to read them, make use of them and draw your own conclusions.

For the sake of clarity, I will indeed only concentrate on a handful of themes, which have led me to see current societal transition in a new light. I first want to list some of the conflicting values our society is facing today. This will lead me to what I consider the main finding of my study, a certain characterisation of this era in time. Finally, I will list some of the ways these forward thinkers I have met, have developed to successfully adapt to this new paradigm.

5.
CONFLICTING VALUES

I mentioned earlier that I see life as a perpetual state of unbalance, very much like walking. Well, society feels to me like walking on a tightrope, always balancing between conflicting values and finding which path prevents us from falling. This has always been the case and today is no exception. We are facing many conflicting dynamics, for example, should we privilege our well-being over planetary boundaries. Obviously, not to use any resources leads to our death and to use them without any concern on their natural replenishment, ends pretty much in the same way. The solution is somewhere in between that spectrum of possibilities. However, that is looking at only one dimension of society. There are many more and my brain starts to hurt when trying to picture an equilibrist walking on an n-dimensional mesh of figurative societal tightropes.

My goal this year was to try and understand the underlying values of recent societal initiatives and see if there were any commonalities or oppositions amongst them. To simplify the complexity of these interdependent systems, I would like to illustrate those findings by describing four of these spectra which I feel are too often overlooked : Utility vs Freedom, Local vs Global, The end of representation vs the need for structure, Inward Change vs Outward Change.

These spectra of societal choices came out of the various interviews I did this year, sometimes, fully fleshed out by one person, at other times, evolving over many conversations with several people along my travels. For this reason and for questions of fluidity, it will be difficult to rightfully attribute authorship of any given idea at every step. However, it is important for me to recognise the generous contributions my interviewees made. Therefore, I invite you again to read the interviews and see for yourself how great minds articulated these thoughts better than I ever could.

Though it may at times feel like I am forecasting futures, this is not my intention. I am merely drawing a line from where existing contemporary trends point today. I am not describing what will be but what could be. If you like a future or oppositely, feel uncomfortable with it, ask yourself why. We always have agency about our future and it is interesting to know why we react in a particular way to an idea. Is it fear of the unknown, caution faced with the unfamiliar, excitement of the new, or a deep ethical concern?

5.1. Utility vs Freedom

One technology which time seems to have come is the self-driving car. Google, Tesla, BMW, Mercedes, Uber and maybe even Amazon [1] are in the race to come up with this technology in the next few years. Though the technology itself and its legal framework still need to be tweaked, the possibilities offered by mass adoption of self-driving vehicles are impressive, in particular, when adding this new idea to existing transportation classics.

Imagine that a car-sharing company owned a fleet of self-driving cars in your city. These cars would be driving around town like taxis and you could flag one

---

1. In November 2015, Amazon filled a patent dealing with the issue or reversible lanes which was awarded in January 2017.

down and get dropped off in front of your destination. The transaction would be seamless thanks to your pre-registered credit card – and probably much cheaper since the cost of a human driver does not reduce over time as fast as technology does. You would be safer, not only from being overcharged, taking the long way home or violence which sadly happens in some countries, but also from traffic accidents. Self-driving cars will communicate between one another as part of the Internet of Things (IoT), and so accidents will be less likely, probably an even greater reduction than that of commercial planes in the last decades, which have always been piloted by highly trained individuals compared to the relatively meagre training we receive to hold a driver's license. Communicating cars will also reduce traffic jams, your itinerary continuously being optimised to avoid them. Traffic congestion today costs American an estimated $124 billion every year[2]. Come to think of it, why not do away with stopping altogether? If cars can communicate, why would you need traffic lights or even a speed limit? Computer models today can already easily handle dense traffic in a twelve-lane motorway no-light intersection without breaking a binary sweat. These more-than-likely *electric* cars will never have to park and will free up more lanes in cities to fluidify traffic or build new homes, pedestrian or bike lanes, or parks. Streets or lanes connected to the IoT, could actually reverse at different times during the day and adapt to traffic conditions. The technology exists and is being trialled for roads to electrically charge the cars while driving on them. If connected to clean energy sources, this could soon reduce our global carbon footprint by 10% which is today

---

2. *50% Rise in gridlock costs by 2030*, INRIX and the Centre for Economics and Business Research

attributed to cars, trucks and buses[3]. Self-driving cars would continuously be used compared to our current individual cars that we use maybe a few hours a day and the rest of the time stay idle, parked somewhere. In terms of resource management, the environment, well-being, security, economic benefit, this future is much brighter!

However, in such a world, will you be able to turn off your GPS? Another self-driving car cannot avoid you if you are not telling it where you are, by giving your GPS location and intended itinerary for example.

Well, for so many benefits, most people would not mind I guess. How about giving up your real-time health data? One could make a pretty convincing case that the same approach would save thousands from dying of flu pandemics each year, or give early warnings in case of heart attacks, or even track sexually transmitted diseases. Stop the AIDS epidemic anyone? The true benefit of such a system really only works when everyone partakes. Not to share your information has a societal cost.

If I drive a car that does not communicate with others, all the other cars will probably have to slow down for security reasons. If I do not share my real-time health data and spread the flu to a dozen co-workers, the economic cost to society – namely their time away from work and medical bills – are all attributable to me. For the greater benefit of society, can I, can you still enjoy privacy?

While at MIT's *Initiative on the Digital Economy*, a PhD candidate mused and told me the following tale. Imagine the 20th century saw the confrontation between democracy and market economies on one side, and centralised regimes and planned economies on the other. And to oversimplify matters, democracy won... or at least, it has up to now. The reasoning behind the success of

---

3. Intergovernmental Panel on Climate Change (IPCC)

market economies – following Friedrich Hayek's theories – is that the information of supply and demand, and need in general, is diffused throughout society and difficult to centralise. For that reason, it is better to leave decision-making to the end customer or the citizen. This leads to market economies and in political systems, we call it democracy. However, today with our consumer data easily accessible and in formats easy to centralise, do these arguments still hold? Would Stalin's (mis-)management of consumer products in the Soviet Union have been such a failure with access to Amazon's sales data? Maybe the 21st century will see the return of authoritarian centralised regimes and planned economies...

This debate on how much freedom we give up to be members of a given society is not new and goes all the way back to the Ancient Greeks, but as Gaspard Koenig explains in his brilliantly concise *Le Révolutionnaire, l'Expert et le Geek*[4], the growing importance of data in our society raises these questions anew. We must be vigilant to decide where on this first spectrum we wish to position ourselves, because Big Brother will not use *1984* television propaganda and the military to secure power, but sleek smart-objects and beautifully designed useful apps.

I – perhaps naively – do not even think there is need for a conspiracy theory. We may enslave ourselves voluntarily and if so, that would be our right as members and makers of society. I am simply not convinced we would all be doing so consciously. Today, our freely given data is only used to generate the impressive revenue stream of such companies as Google or Facebook. When our data starts to be used for saving lives in society and not just generating revenue in the private sector, it may no longer be as simple to "unregister".

---

4. The Revolutionary, the Expert and the Geek.

5.2. Local vs Global

For the last few decades, the "Holy Grail" of physics has been to develop a so-called Unified Theory. Although astrophysicists actually and admittedly only understand roughly 4% of the visible universe[5], the rules governing all these large objects is quite well understood and the models used predict very precisely the movements and interactions of planets, galaxies and "large" objects like pebbles or us humans. On the other side of the spectrum, quantum mechanics explains how fundamental particles (atoms, photons, electrons, quarks, etc.) interact and the forces that govern them with remarkable precision. The main issue is bridging the gap. At a certain scale, both models fail to blend seamlessly into one. However, scientist instinctively believe that there must be an overarching theory that makes sense of it all : A Unified Theory. In a way, we currently understand how a knight and a rook can move on a chess board but not that they are pieces of a game call chess. We humans today are faced with a similar conundrum when it comes to societal change.

Though introspection, neurology and human psychology may give us a certain understanding of how we individually make decisions at a local scale, and economics and anthropology at greater scales, the rules governing one scale do not transition seamlessly to the other. Subsidising the oil industry in the Gulf of Mexico may make sense locally for jobs, but globally, the subsidisation of the carbon industry may slow down the adoption of more environmentally sustainable solutions and may be detrimental to all, including inhabitants of Houston, TX. This problem of bridging

---

5. Most of the Universe seems to be made out of Dark Matter (~20% of the universe's mass) and Dark Energy which is a force that repels gravity (~75% of the universe's mass). The word "Dark" here meaning "we don't really know yet what this stuff is".

both sides of the spectrum has two main causes. The first is that consequences of decisions at any one scale in regards to other scales, are too complex for us to fully comprehend. The second is that we do not have measurement equivalencies between otherwise connected systems : in this case, the economy and the environment are connected but how do you choose between either? How can you compare dollars per capita and atmospheric carbon content?

Though these two issues are problematic enough, the cause for the biggest challenges on the local and global spectrum are due to not making decisions at every scale of a given problem. Indeed, for solutions to work, the given problem needs to be tackled at every scale where it exists. If you take racism for example, a national solution, such as the Emancipation Proclamation in the United States, did only improve in part the problem of race in America before it was translated at much more local and even individual levels, during the Civil Rights movements of the 1960s. Still today, the issue of racism needs to be dealt with at both individual and institutional levels.

We live in a world where the economy and the environment are global systems but where the Political is national or sub-national. This situation is the cause of today's biggest issues. Though, I will mainly give environmental examples because of our familiarity with them, Climate Change is not by any means the only global issue we face today. The automation of the economy which could in a couple of decades make most of us redundant and unemployable, is another great global issue faced with the same shortcoming of scale [6]. So are many ethical

---

6. Automation as it is happening could be very positive for a small proportion of Humanity but detrimental to most, similar to when Humanity moved from a hunter-gatherer society to farming. That change initially was detrimental to the diets of most humans and only better for a handful. This point is very well argued by Yuval Noah Harari in his 2011 book, *Sapiens :*

dilemmas that deal with technology such as Artificial Intelligence, transhumanism, artificial life, customisable offspring, to name but a few. Two options exist to overcome this problem : re-nationalising the economy or globalising politics.

Scaling down the economy to a national level is the choice current populist movements have opted for. However, on top of being anachronistic as I have explained previously, this approach is flawed for two other reasons. The first is that environmental problems cannot be nationalised, since the planet functions as a global ecosystem. It is no wonder that nearly all nationalistic movement leaders are climate change deniers. Since there is no national solution to the environmental problem, the easiest and really only approach you can take is to deny the existence of the problem altogether[7].

Nationalists may argue that individual States agree regularly with one another and so, nationalism is not incompatible with solutions at a global scale. Recent history is indeed full of examples of bilateral or even multilateral trade agreements, for example. This is true, but such cases usually have win-win solutions, compatible with nations putting forward their own interest first. However, this no longer functions when faced with a lose-lose or no-win scenario. A common example of which

---

A Brief History of Humankind. In his writings, Harari convincingly explains that agriculture was a trap humanity walked unknowingly into and from which there was no coming back. Once down the path of agriculture and specialisation, it is nigh-impossible to return to a hunter-gatherer society. The increase in resources offered by agriculture leads to an increase in population, which in turns puts more pressure on resources to the point where hunting and gathering would no longer cover the needs of the population. So even if early agriculture of a small number of crops lead to poorer diets for humanity, once the first seed planted there was no turning back. The various global issues I list here-above could constitute similar traps we are walking unknowingly into.

7. On Thursday, June 1st 2017, Donald Trump declared that the United States would leave the Paris Accords on Climate Change. His justification was that he had been elected by "the inhabitants of Pittsburgh and not Paris". This is quite true but he seemingly forgets that inhabitants of Pittsburgh are also inhabitants of the Planet Earth.

is the classic Prisoner's Dilemma, which most basic version reads as follows :

Two criminals are caught by the police after a robbery. Unfortunately, the police do not have enough proof to convict them. So, they place each robber in separate interrogation rooms and give them a choice : If they confess that the robber in the other room committed the crime, then they themselves walk free and the other goes to jail. Four possibilities arise from this choice :

— Both robbers attest that the other committed the crime, they both go to jail.

— Robber A tells on Robber B and B says nothing about A. A walks free, B goes to jail.

— Robber B tells on Robber A and A says nothing about B. B walks free, A goes to jail.

— Neither robber tells on the other. They both walk free.

The best scenario for the robbers is for both to stay quiet but this only can occur if they trust each other. Honour amongst thieves if you will.

The problems we face today are often of this nature. It would probably better for all if we started taxing carbon more and disinvesting from carbon-intensive companies and processes. However, our industries being highly reliant on fossil energy, to do so would cost a lot to businesses (actually, consumers at the end of the day but let's simplify). So, if a single country started to do so, industry there may move to a country with lower carbon taxes. Since countries compete for industry implantation, global carbon taxes and the end of oil subsidies have trouble becoming a reality. For such a scenario to function – i.e. for nationalistic states to improve the global situation in a lose-lose scenario – it would require a great amount of trust. And trust does not happen between closed off nations.

The second issue when opting for the nationalist approach is that History has shown us again and again, that isolationism is an overall bad strategy if other nations decide to maintain openness. As I have alluded to previously, in the 11th century when the Arab Empire decided to close itself off from the rest of the world or when China did the same in the 15th century, both regions were respectively much more advanced than other nations, European nations in particular. However, a couple of centuries later, they found themselves behind the curb and were easily conquered by nations having maintained trade and openness to one another. Though some people – even maybe a majority – in so-called developed nations, feel like globalisation has been detrimental of late to their lives and choose to opt for nationalism, globalisation has improved the lives of many more people worldwide, and these people have no reason to close themselves off. It is likely that the same historical mechanisms would apply again and even the most advanced nations today would not maintain their privileged positions by closing themselves off to the rest of the world. This time, however, given the speed of information creation and exchange, the loss of their relatively advantageous positions might be much swifter.

While in Japan, I met with Professor Kanji Tanimoto[8] of Waseda University, who illustrated this very point by telling me about his country's somewhat singular corporate culture. A specialist in business and society, Professor Tanimoto illustrated his point by telling me about his contract with Waseda University, or lack thereof :

"Did you know that we rarely have written employment contracts in Japan ? You are sitting in my office at Waseda

---

8. See Kanji Tanimoto's interview on the study's website.

University and I teach classes here but I have no written contract with the university, no job description. People define their job within a small group of their colleagues, taking care to avoid conflicts. They don't talk explicitly about objectives and responsibilities. They infer a lot and imagine what their colleagues would think if they did something within the team. To work in this vague, highly implicit and loose structure, you need a strong cultural cohesiveness, which is why Japanese companies only hire classical Japanese students and international exposure is actually sometimes seen as a drawback

[...]

The difficulty for the Japanese [...] is that they lack international and external experiences enabling [a] more open and global identity definition process to occur. This prevents them from tackling issues in a global way, which is very important today, and is in itself a hurdle for them to change this. International exposure gives you perspective on your own culture and helps you to make it evolve. [...] It will be a difficult challenge to tackle but a necessary one for Japan to stay relevant in the world."

Consequently, I believe the only solution may be to globalise politics. This will not be an easy task though, because our systems do not encourage such a solution. Most Nation-States are structured in such a way that the ability to transfer power is in the hands of the head of state. For this reason, the people in power need to voluntarily reduce their own power. Another no-win scenario, which in part is the problem plaguing the United Nations, the European Union or any supra-national organisation. Examples in History are rare, when people fought to come into power only to relinquish some of it. This being said, a phenomenon making the whole Global-Local spectrum more complex, may offer a way out of this corner we find ourselves painted into.

The concept of localism today may no longer be geographical. In the past months, I have met more like-minded people working in cafés in San Francisco, Medellin, London, Helsinki, Nairobi, Beijing and Bali than in my own apartment building in Paris. And for those afraid the culture and way of life of developed nations is in jeopardy, the same feeling is true in the developing world, as Paul Mugambi[9], the CEO of Kytabu, an innovative EdTech startup, passionately recounted to me :

"I feel I have become a clone of just another guy from the First World. I'm just like you. In this process, I maybe have lost my values, the values my grandparents stood for. We had so many traditions : the first bath of a child, the naming of a child, we had so many functions and small celebrations. During the harvest season, we would celebrate in a particular way, including having sex, which would have an impact on the country's birth rate. We had more solidarity. I have family members in town who live 30 minutes away from my home but whom I haven't talked to in 5 years. We just send "Happy Birthday" on Whatsapp groups. One of my sisters lives in London, a cousin in Canada.

When we meet as a group, there is this feeling of recognition of who we really are. I believe we are losing something of value. The world is becoming uniform and that is not interesting. As a foreigner, you are here in this café with me and the menu is similar to most of what you would find anywhere in the world. You're not able to try Kenyan food.

A lot of our problems are solved through technology but there is a high-priced trade-off. And I am also creating this change because recently I proposed that my mother move to the city with me so she can live an easier life that the one she is leading in the country."

---

9. See Paul Mugambi's interview on the study's website.

The global-local spectrum is difficult because across the layers of community one feels allegiance to, one must find the self. As Gaspard Koenig puts it :

"With digital tools, one can create multiple communities. Localism today does not any longer have any geographical meaning and does not have to be anchored in one territory, under one homogeneous representative political system. It offers the possibility to belong to multicultural groups.

[...]. In effect, [people] create their identity by layering their affiliation to various groups and identities which seem – to a certain extent at least – chosen. To truly chose, one must be educated and have enough means to do so, but that is another question entirely."

More recently, in Wellington, I met with Joshua Vial of *Enspiral*[10], an innovative organisation structured as a cooperative of entrepreneurs. Though most of the members are Wellingtonians, many of them come from other cities in New Zealand or even other countries. *Enspiral* works hard to create a common culture and shared principles but as Joshua explained to me, paraphrasing research from Clay Shirky : *"when the cost of transacting information goes through the floor, then command-and-control hierarchical structures become less efficient than network-based organisations"*. With today's digital tools, networks no longer need to be fully geographically local and so the local / global ("glocal") debate gets this much more interesting. Some believe that the way we will achieve global decision-making may be through the scaling of non-geographically local networks, which offer the adequate trust for no-win problems to be solved. It is still unclear if trust can scale globally, but users of networked platforms like Airbnb or Uber, already welcome into their homes or are willing to enter the cars

---

10. See Joshua Vial's interview on the study's website.

of perfect strangers, which in a way is encouraging.

Finally, if our institutions and societal processes are no longer in tune with our experience of space, the same assessment can be made of time. Cumulatively slow processes like greenhouse gas emissions, require humans to think in unnatural abstract timeframes of decades and even centuries. Timescales that today contradict the incentive structures of our political and corporate systems. On the opposite side of the time spectrum our "real time" media cycle stifles critical thinking and reflexion, dooming most of us to either ignore information altogether or desperately re-act to events we do not begin to comprehend. For our survival, it will be imperative to find ways to tackle issues not only at every needed spatial scale but at every time scale as well.

The "*glocal* spectrum" of choices is complex but vital, if humanity wishes to overcome the main systemic issues threatening its survival and way of life today. This will be achieved by better understanding the interactions between local and global decisions and their consequences, as well as by addressing issues at every scale along the spectrum, including the global scale. We will also need to build more equivalencies between connected domains such as economic growth, the environment and social well-being. "Local" no longer being necessarily a geographical term, we must face the complexity of a multi-layering effect of identities, which may surprisingly also be the solution to many of our problems. We will also need to integrate multiple timescales to our processes, making sure that we are not over focusing on the present and dooming the future. Only by realising and embracing all this complexity, can we hope to achieve this "Unified theory" of decision-making.

5.3. The End of Representation vs The Need for Structure

Let's play a game. On July 20th 1969, Neil Armstrong and Buzz Aldrin were the first two men to set foot on the Moon. However, to take that giant step for mankind, how many people do you think directly contributed? Ballpark figure

— The current number of NASA employees : 17,345 [11]

— The number of people working for the American Congress : 23,971 [12]

— The number of employees at General Motors, a company making roughly 10'000'000 vehicles a year : 212,000 [13]

The answer is roughly 400,000 [14]. As I have mentioned several times already, the complex accomplishments of the industrial era, like landing or the Moon, building millions of cars every year through a complex global supply chain, or simply the existence of efficient Nation States, were made possible through large complex organisations utilising systems of representation, hierarchical structures chief among them. However, today, with complexity having increased even more – remember this is a good thing – hierarchical organisations are reaching their limits.

For the five years prior to this study, I worked for the Research & Development Department of EDF, the world's second-largest power utility. EDF has the largest research capability of any energy company worldwide. It boasts an impressive +2'000 researchers with an annual budget of over half a billion euros. However, even with all these in-house specialists, EDF does not have all the expertise

---

11. "NASA workforce profile". NASA. January 11, 2011. *Retrieved December 17, 2012.*

12. In the year 2000, there were approximately 11,692 personal staff, 2,492 committee staff, 274 leadership staff, 5,034 institutional staff, and 3,500 GAO employees, 747 CRS employees, and 232 CBO employees.

13. GM annual report 2014

14. *Team Moon : How 400,000 People Landed Apollo 11 on the Moon,* Catherine Thimmesh, 2015

it requires to fully understand today's energy sector and needs to look outside the company. This is in part, why I helped create their Open Innovation Team and corporate venture capital fund.

Not only has the world become more complex, but with improvements in digital technologies and the reduction in transactional costs, as Joshua Vial explained in the previous section, it is more effective to create networks than large hierarchical organisations. Furthermore, hierarchical organisations have been optimised over decades to achieve their tasks ever more efficiently. Like the Tyrannosaurus Rex evolving over millennia to become a super-efficient killing machine and then being wiped out by the Cretaceous–Tertiary crisis, hierarchical optimisation unfortunately makes large organisations less flexible, which sadly for them seems to be the most important quality to have in our fast-changing era.

Many people have started to realise these shortcomings and are gradually calling for more direct forms of decision-making and organisational structures. Of late, there has been a renewed interest in Direct Democracy [15], Liquid Democracy [16] and Sortition [17], in the public sector, and cooperatives and non-hierarchical corporate structures are blossoming [18]. This apparent downfall of hierarchy has even led some to question the representativeness of the most iconic hierarchical

---

15. Today, most western democracies are highly representative. Citizens are represented at various levels of government and in different branches of government by elected or named officials (mayors, members of parliament, governors, ministers, presidents, etc.). Direct Democracy is a form or disintermediated democracy.

16. A form of democracy where the electorate gives voting power to delegates rather than representatives.

17. Sortition is a political process where officials are selected randomly from a larger pool of candidates. This is how most juries in democracies are chosen.

18. According to Michel Bauwens, a Belgian Economist specialised in Commons (see his interview on the study's website), the number of cooperatives in Europe has been multiplied by 10 in the last 10 years.

structure : The Nation State. In 2014, utilising Blockchain technology, Susanne Tarkowski Tempelhof created *Bitnation*, the world's first "Virtual Nation". *Bitnation* is the *"first operational decentralized borderless voluntary nation, and provides its "citizens" the same services as traditional governments : a secure identification system, dispute resolution, security and insurance"*. More recently, in October 2016, Dr. Igor Ashurbeyli founded *Asgardia*, the first "Space Nation" which, until it builds its giant orbital space-station, or space-nation, is in effect another virtual nation of 170'000 certified citizens, at the moment of writing.

As I said earlier in this essay, I may feel closer in my values and ideals to some people I have in cafés along my journey than other French people or New Zealanders, people with whom I proudly share citizenship. Moreover, self-determination, a corner stone of our international law, is not dependent on land and states that, based on the principal of equal rights and fair equality of opportunity, peoples have the right to freely choose their sovereignty and international political status with no interference. This may seem to some like science fiction, but what is stopping me today from creating a nation of like-minded people with our own laws, constitution and tax system? All this, up to very recently, would have required huge resources and an immense bureaucracy but today, an app could allocate funds collected online quite simply and efficiently with direct decision-making from citizens of the virtual state, without corruption and informational loss because of an imperfect representative system. Maybe this could even be the way to solve the local vs global dilemma I alluded to beforehand.

These new technological abilities are exciting and could help solve many issues of our current organisational systems. However, while the thrill of empowerment and freedom runs through our social body, we should be wary not to throw out the baby of existing rights with the proverbial bath water.

We should not forget all that the Ancient Greeks and philosophers of the Enlightenment gave us as a foundation for our organisational thinking. Though I have not heard people defend this view of late, when Direct and Liquid Democracies started their recent "buzz-word phase", some thought it would be easy to create digital tools to record the needs and desires of individual citizens, the sum of which would constitute the Will of the People. The simplicity of this idea is very appealing, but I maintain we should defend and be proud of complexity. Over a quarter of a millennium ago, Rousseau in his *Contrat Social*, warned us that citizens should not only consider their own interest but aspire to a vision of a society they wish to belong to : the common good [19].

Silicon Valley should maybe revisit the contributions of these, sometimes forgotten, great thinkers before building new tools which quite likely lead to formerly met and avoided organisational pitfalls. For example, Uber takes advantage of the reduced transactional costs offered by technology. However, the global car-sharing company does not employ its drivers, considering them users of their platform. While allowing the company to drastically reduce the cost of car rides in most cities in the world, this approach also flies at the face of two hundred years of social battles by unions and workers to earn legal rights and social security. The novelty of Uber's great user

---

19. I cite a short passage of Rousseau's for the efficiency and beauty with which he writes : " Il y a souvent bien de la différence entre la volonté de tous et la volonté générale; celle-ci ne regarde qu'à l'intérêt commun; l'autre regarde à l'intérêt privé, et n'est qu'une somme des volontés particulières : mais ôtez de ces mêmes volontés les plus et les moins qui s'entre-détruisent, reste pour somme des différences la volonté générale ". Rousseau; *Du Contrat Social*

experience hides that the company's model is far from being as innovative. Some have compared the economic model to "neo-serfdom"[20].

Finally, I asked what could stop me creating a Virtual State today. Well, the answer is that such a networked form of governance – though highly interesting, maybe appealing and worthy of exploration – is dependent on basic freedoms of assembly, mobility and free speech, all guaranteed by existing Nation States.

There exists a strong trend to create a world of freelancers working project to project, nations of one defined by a layering of communities defining our identity, but we must be careful not to deny our social nature. New technology and our overall education level may enable us to shed some representation, grow in our responsibilities, and step closer to the more ideal models of society such as Direct Democracy. However, we still *need* structure and society. Humanity has spent millennia building structures enabling communal life and avoiding its pitfalls. We must not be too quick to judge the past and not forget why things are the way they are. To find the solutions in this spectrum of choice, we must hoist ourselves on the shoulders of giants and not cut their legs out under them.

5.4. Inward Change vs Outward Change

Between 2002 and 2012, the number of Americans practicing yoga and meditation doubled[21]. Google and other companies battling for the best and brightest started offering free classes to their employees around the same

---

20. There are many examples of such claims and so not to be labelled a communist, I will simply cite the quite non-communist *Financial Times*, in a 2016 article. *Uberisation and the dangers of neo-serfdom*, Rana Foroohar, August 10th 2016
21. National Health Interview Survey (NHIS)

time and it has since become a standard perk in Silicon Valley. Though a minority movement, Minimalism – the practice of reducing one's material possessions to increase one's freedom and general well-being – is on the rise amongst Millennials, as indicated by the growing millions of subscribers to blogs like *Mr. Money Mustache* or *TheMinimalists*, as well as the growing number of Digital Nomads roaming the planet with little more than a backpack. The self-help industry has grown at average annual rate of 6% since the financial crisis, and is projected to continue to do so in the next few years [22]. Maybe due to the perceptions of uncertain times, even in my highly secular birth country of France [23], there is an increase in religiosity among the young [24]. Share The World's Resources (STWR), a London-based organisation [25], is trying to promote increased empathy and sharing among people to help solve our global issues. Schumacher College [26], a progressive higher education institution in Devon, developed its curriculum following the oriental precept that *"people achieve abundance not through accumulation of wealth but by reducing their needs"*.

Maybe faced with the complexity of our world, it seems people are focusing more on themselves, or maybe and more positively, people are realising that as an island species we must adapt to the environment around us more than change the environment to suit our needs. Regardless of the reason, there is an undeniable tendency

---

22. Marketdata Enterprise Inc.

23. France is 54% agnostic or atheist (Corref 2015)

24. LaCroix and Opinionway June 2016 Study. In 2016, 46% of young people (18 to 30-year-olds) said they believed in God (in 2008, this number was 38%), compared to a national average of 38%. To dispel any potential preconceptions, this increase in religiosity is not due to an "islamisation" of the population. According to the French Ministry of the Interior, each year around 4000 people convert to Islam and between 4000 to 7000 to Christian faiths.

25. See Adam Parsons' interview on the study's website

26. See Jonathan Dawson's interview on the study's website.

for inward change among developed nations. I like to think optimistically that it is Humanity's way of entering adulthood. Whereas children and teenagers test boundaries to define themselves, usually by breaking objects or rules, adults, more confident about who they are, try to find their position in the greater environment that surrounds them. Humanity started with breaking rocks to form tools, and smashing atoms together to understand the make-up of the universe, and maybe today, we feel confident enough about our basic understanding of the world, to look within and start to focus on adapting to the environment more so than it having to change for us.

This trend is yet too marginal to draw any conclusions, but it does slightly depart from Humanity's dominant historical approach to change. Many scientists believe that unlike any other living creature on Earth, humanity has managed to slow down the basic evolutionary process of natural selection through its ingenuity, and maybe even now, is starting to set its own rules of evolution.

With advances in genetics and gene selection, we may soon be able to choose the genes and traits of our children. Though still science fiction at this stage – several organisations are working on brain-machine interfaces similar to what was shown in *The Matrix*[27]. In the next few decades we may be able to supplement our existing memory with storage capacity in the cloud and our existing knowledge with direct brain access to the internet. Some advanced prosthetics are today being connected to patients' nervous systems, so that thinking a movement actually makes the prosthetic act as willed. After a long legal battle, Oscar Pistorious, a double leg amputee from South Africa, was allowed to compete in the 2012 Olympic

---

27. For example, Elon Musk, the CEO of *Tesla Motors* and *SpaceX*, founded *Neuralink* in 2016 and first publicly reported its existence in March 2017.

Games. Though he did not win any medals, the speed of technological advancement outpacing natural evolution, it is only a matter of time before "enhanced" humans outrun, outjump, and overall outperform "basic model" humans.

Transhumanism, the movement to enhance human intellectual, physical and psychological capabilities through technology, also follows this trend of us changing ourselves from within and not the environment around us. We are not there yet, but we may in the next few decades be faced with deep questions about what exactly constitutes a human being. After how many improvements to our body or mind, will we consider an individual no longer part of the Human species? Human ingenuity implies that there are few limits to this path. Maybe some distant day in the future, we may consider our source of energy (food) to be inefficient and too wasteful of the planet's resources, at which point maybe we will be inclined to modify ourselves to gain the ability of plants to photosynthesize and draw our energy directly from sunlight.

I realise this is pure science fiction and not the focus of my study but the questions of transhumanism are far reaching. Many people, including great thinkers such as physicist Stephen Hawking, are afraid of the emergence of Artificial Intelligence (A.I.) and its eventual hypothetical genocide of Humanity. Others believe A.I. will help humanity overcome our current issues. Like most people I have no idea about such matters, but looking at this relatively new trend of changing ourselves to adapt to our environment, I think there is a possibility that humanity may be tempted to meld with A.I. and maybe become some new species altogether. From slowing down natural selection, to devising the selection ourselves, we may end up defining and designing our own species altogether.

I do not wish to turn this essay into a catalogue of science-fiction what-ifs (some of which though more science than fiction), but I wanted to illustrate the implications of the inward-facing change trend. We may be seeing the start of a new age of maturity for Humanity, a gradual end to our destructive influence on the planet, but it will also lead to some unsettling ethical questions about who we are and what constitutes being human. Furthermore, though I strongly believe we have neglected our adaptation to the exterior up to now and this trend is to be encouraged, there are many issues that require Human intervention, at the very least solving man-made problems. Newly found inner peace should not make us complacent of these situations. We should not retreat from our responsibilities to civic life, the environment, or human ideals such as human dignity.

The pendulum between internal and external change may have swung for too long in one direction and today, a return to the centre may be exactly what we need. However, we must be careful not to withdraw from our responsibilities and be wary of the possible implications to our species' identity.

In these four spectra : Utility vs Freedom, the end of Representation vs the Need for Structure, Global vs Local and Inward vs Outward change, my aim was not to say where we should land on each specific issue. I admit quite honestly being utterly incapable of doing so anyway. The reason I chose to describe these four dimensions, was to illustrate different perspectives we can have on the transition we are living through. Once again, I have chosen a limited number and society is currently balancing on many other "tightropes", but I felt these four are often overlooked compared to more debated ones such as Development vs Sustainability. My study started by exploring the underlying values of the current societal transition. I felt that making a list of intrinsically arguable values from my research was less interesting than to show often implicit social spectra, on which to question our own values. The questions raised by them are difficult and that realisation led me to what I consider the main finding of my study : The Age of Transition.

6.
THE AGE OF TRANSITION

To help us make sense of this world, we humans tend to privilege clear categories and stable states. We know in reality, that everything is interconnected and in constant evolution, but it is easier – and in fact, the only actionable possibility for our finite brains – to think in successive fixed frames of limited complexity. In Chemistry, we learn that different molecules interact to create new ones and we implicitly focus on the initial state of distinct molecules and the end result of the reaction. In Biology, the appeal of stable states is probably in part responsible for the considerable number of creationists around the world[1]. In History, we learn that Antiquity is followed by the Middle Ages, which in turn, changes into the Renaissance. Even apparent tipping points hide more progressive changes. The storming of the Bastille on July 14th 1789, is the emblematic date of the French Revolution, often considered the death knell of French monarchy and the birth of the French Republic. Well, even without considering the run-up to the 1789 Revolution and the fact that *La Révolution* lasted at least until 1793, the following decades saw France live through two additional revolutions (1830 and 1848), two Republics,

---

1. Though most often thought of as a debate only in the United States, a 2010 poll by Ipsos for Reuters News in 24 countries, showed that overall 28% of peopled questioned identified as creationists. The "evolutionist" view was most popular in Sweden (68%), Germany (65%), and China (64%), with the United States ranking 18th (28%), between Mexico (34%) and Russia (26%); the "creationist" view was most popular in Saudi Arabia (75%), Turkey (60%), and Indonesia (57%), with the United States ranking 6th (40%), between Brazil (47%) and Russia (34%).

two Empires, two Constitutional Monarchies, and only in 1870, did France politically settle on its Third Republic, which indeed lasted seven decades until the German Occupation of France in 1940. Times of transition are not only important but are often overlooked and somewhat forgotten. Without clear examples in memory, it makes it more difficult for us to know how to successfully live through a time of accelerated change.

I myself was affected by this bias when designing my study. As mentioned previously, my aim was to find common values in recent initiatives so as to maybe, discover our aspirations for the next stable societal state of society. Though not necessarily believing in a future stable state of society or even believing that such a thing ever existed, I thought that better understanding those aspirations could give direction to the change we are living through. By knowing the direction, we could transition faster. However, over the year, I realised that my greatest finding was that this question did not matter much. The future matters less than the present. Transition is a time in itself and not a lost parenthesis wedged between important periods.

The perspective of consecutive stable states not only undermines the importance of transitional periods and strips them from our collective memory, it also gives us the impression that historical periods emerge somewhat organically when the time is "right"; that mostly, change is out of our control. This is to some extent true, but it hides the reality that those organic movements are made of the active choices of any number of individuals. Rosa Parks was neither the first person or the last who refused to move to the back of the bus and though her decision for some unfathomable, organic and great reason, crystallised in our minds and the minds of people at the time, I would argue that hers was no more important or less so that the previous and following refusals. **To successfully transition, we need to be able to decide on what we want for ourselves and our future. Sadly, what this year has led me to understand is that we are terribly underprepared to make such decisions**.

The 19th and 20th centuries saw huge societal changed as I tried to illustrate previously, but were in large part governed by one single rule : production. More was simply better. Today, there is no one hegemonic societal driver. We are faced with several competing imperatives, including production and growth but also the environment and social connectivity. Regardless of what these different governing dynamics are actually, the fact that there is now more than one, means we need to arbitrate between them. As individuals, we need to decide which mix makes sense to us. Oversimplistically, what is more important a nicer car, free time to spend with my family or meaning in my job? At a time, maybe the bigger house, the nicer car, the bigger TV, was the obvious choice but this no longer is the case. Corporations up to now have been focused on *how* questions : how to grow, how to produce more, sell more, make greater profit margins, acquire market shares. Entire strategy departments and the global strategy consulting market is devoted to answering these difficult questions. However, few companies ask the question of *why* they exist ; given all their employees and assets, what is their purpose in society. Even fewer companies are structured to answer these questions.

Though it was probably a necessity, the increased importance of representation and expertise in decision-making has alienated most people from having to deal with complexity in their day to day lives. The vast majority of us do not make the complex decisions involved with energy, infrastructure, international trade, ethics, urbanism, the financial world, technology, etc. However, as I alluded to before, complexity has reached a level where even experts cannot forecast how their decisions will pan out and so we need to change our organisations to reflect this new reality and solve that issue. We need to accept that we cannot predict some outcomes, decide together regardless on which direction to take, and shoulder collectively the responsibility of moving forward into the unknown.

As individuals, our education system still oftentimes focuses on knowledge but not on how to question what is important to us individually, how to evaluate rational arguments, listen to and explicit gut instincts, to critically question existing systems, imagine new ones, be faced with the failure of our first ideas and how to overcome the disappointment [2], to defend our point of view and gather others to our cause. We are taught mostly what to know and not how to think, feel and intuit.

As I tried to show through the four spectra I described, we have difficult decisions to make right now and in the future. Decisions as individuals, as organisations and as communities, including nation-states and as a global species. We are simply not used to struggle with such complex questions and are not prepared to do so. To illustrate what I mean, with all its complexity and far-reaching implications, Brexit should not have been an

---

2. In every creative undertaking, we are faced with the realisation that somebody has already somehow done what you thought was your original and novel idea. When designing this study, I initially thought, I would go around the world and find examples of solutions to our global issues. Then in October of 2015, four months before I was to set off on my study, the French documentary *Demain* came out for the COP21 in Paris. That documentary, which I greatly recommend, does exactly what I initially wanted to do, better than I ever could. The team behind the documentary had more funding, a professional camera crew, a big star attached to the project (Mélanie Laurent), Cyril Dion's contacts of A-list change makers across the world... In every respect, this was what I wanted to do, simply done better. I had to change my project, reframe or pivot as "creatives" like to say. That ability is an important aspect of the creative process and one that is rarely taught in schools.

all of nothing, one time, yes/no question. And though I have a personal opinion on the issue, I happily admit that nobody knows what the right decision was on such a complex and complicated question. The issue is not with the general public's intelligence, or lack of, as you sometimes hear. Even if it were, the system I feel should adapt to our humanity, if not what use is it to us? Society is for its members and it is simply badly designed if it does not serve this purpose. However, this also means that as individuals, we do have a responsibility to adapt and conform to a reasonable measure so as to be part of society.

I believe, our struggles today are due to inappropriate education and structures, and a lack of practice. The United Kingdom, an illustrative example of a normal Western Democracy on such issues, before the vote on Brexit, only had two national referenda in the last 50 years, so over the last two generations of its citizens : The 1975 European Communities membership referendum and the 2011 Alternative Vote referendum. A Swiss citizen, during the same period, could have chosen to take part in 171 federal votes [3]. The lack of practice of most democracies generally leads to emotional reactionary votes which do not focus on the issues and end up being a popularity vote of the current government. We should simply change the system to avoid such foreseeable problems. Let us also just remind ourselves that if citizens are incapable of deciding on issues, even if there is no institutional obstacle for them to do so, then there is no democracy.

This transition is an age in itself, where there is no one hegemonic way of thinking. This forces us to decide what we want for society as individuals, corporations, governments, and as a species. To successfully manage this transition, I believe we need to build up our capacity for

---

3. The Swiss Federal Council Website

complex decision-making at all levels. We need to take control of our future narrative and act to make it a reality. The future does not just happen, it is built. And first, we need to learn how to decide on the future we desire in this complex time in our History.

You may well ask how we can learn how to decide. The last part of this study explores the solutions I have seen and discussed along the way, to gain this ability to decide and successfully live through a time of transition.

7.
LEARNING TO DECIDE

Faced with unprecedently complex decisions at all levels of society, we must remember that, as I see it, we should be proud to be faced with such challenges. It denotes all the challenges we have already overcome and all that we have learned to arrive at this juncture. Most of these issues are not new, we just until recently were oblivious to their existence. They are just new to us. Yes, we are underprepared for overcoming these challenges, but that has always been the case faced with novelty. Thankfully, some pioneers have already started developing ways to improve our decision-making abilities. The following are examples I have come across this year which will hopefully inspire you and give you ideas on how to better take up the challenge laid before you and all of us.

7.1. Trying is Doing

In *Star Wars V : The Empire Strikes Back*, Yoda, the greatest living Jedi Master, tells his pupil Luke Skywalker : "Do or do not, there is no try". With all deference to his great wisdom, what Yoda proposes to master the force is the opposite of what we need to do today. We need to escape this binary approach to action and see it as a continuum of trying, learning and achieving.

As I stated previously, I believe complexity is such that legitimacy to act is no longer given by expertise. Do not get me wrong, knowledge and experience are key, but they can no longer be absolute. There are too many moving parts to most issues for anyone, no matter how bright or educated, to foresee accurately how an action will pan out. This means that the approach to preparation before action no longer functions. Instead, we should design trials that are both the first steps of actions and a source for information to better act – by which I mean try – again afterwards. **We should learn by doing and do by learning**.

My travels took me to Finland, where starting in 2017, the country is trialling a policy of Basic Income. Universal Basic Income is one of these ideas whose time seems to have arrived. An idea originally attributed to Thomas Paine at the end of the 18th century, it has become a buzzword in many developed nations [1], in the last few years. Universal Basic Income (UBI) can be most easily understood as a form of social security system, in which all citizens or residents of a community (most often a country but also regions or cities) regularly receive a set but unconditional sum of money from the public government, regardless of any other income the citizen may receive from any other means.

Though maybe not the first reason people cite, the real underlying reason for the popularity of UBI, when talking to theorists, seems to me to be necessity. The current social security systems of Western nations are being gradually and structurally pushed to a breaking point and we need to change them.

These social security programs were built on the same logic as insurance. They were designed to help people

---

1. Though I am concentrating on First World nations, the logic of Basic Income (and of experimentation) can also, of course, apply to the developing world, as exemplified by *GiveDirectly*. The now important aid NGO started when a group of grad students pooled a few thousand dollars together and distributed the money directly and without any conditions, to Kenyan farmers, monitoring the results. This one experiment comforted them to go against the main Aid World consensus and grow into being an effective organisation in several countries in Sub-Sahara African.

get back on their feet during brief and rare periods of unemployment. The norm was being employed and paying into the system (mainly through income and corporate taxes). In return, one could call on the system when in need or towards the end of one's life when retiring, after having paid into the system for several decades. As Andrew McAfee and Erik Brynjolfsson explain in detail in *The Second Machine Age*, automation is undermining job security at an unprecedented rate. There have been many such studies but just to cite one, the University of Oxford published in 2013[2] an estimate that 47% of jobs will be automated in the next 20 years and no government is prepared for such a change[3]. UBI appears to be a way to maybe stop mass pauperisation in developed nations.

However, Universal Basic Income, is one of these highly complex solutions which cannot be studied beforehand and then decided upon for implementation. Here are just a few of the moving parts that such a policy would impact :

— Universal : Should multimillionaires get it? Immigrants? Minors? In a global society, should you pay other more underprivileged nationalities in other countries? Depending on your answer, you will now impact the ministry of interior and your country's immigration policy and possibly though unlikely, its foreign aid.

— Basic : Food and lodging for sure but do we consider healthcare and education, maybe the access to the internet as basic needs today? Again, depending on

---

2. *The Future Of Employment : How Susceptible Are Jobs To Computerisation ?*, Carl Benedikt Frey and Michael A. Osborne, September 17, 2013

3. In only one country I travelled to did I have the sense that the topic of automation was part of the national discourse : Japan. In my interview of Hitoshi Suzuki, the Corporate Social Responsibility General Manager of NEC – which I encourage you to read on the study's website – he told me that "*Japan is facing a quickly ageing population and will be faced in the future with a real labour shortage issue. For this reason, automation is seen as a good thing here*". In every other country, I was told that the topic of automation was not discussed in the public arena.

your answer, the amount of the Basic Income would vary hugely and potentially impact not only the tax and social benefit system of your country but also the educational framework, the housing industry and healthcare sector.

— How do you pay for it? Through income tax? In a world where automation may eradicate a growing number of jobs, that seems maybe short-sighted. Maybe we should tax capital. Why not? But as explained with the Prisoner's Dilemma in a previous section. This would require nearly complete international coordination.

— Will people still contribute to society if they no longer need to work to survive? This is a true concern for many. The work ethic is so engrained in our society, that money for nothing seems to some like a sure way to create a whole population of "free-loaders" passively watching TV all day long [4].

These are just four complex questions raised by such a policy, and all these interact with one another as well, of course. However, these are also some of the easily foreseeable questions. There also are all the unexpected effects of such a decision.

In 1971, during his second State of the Union address, President Nixon unveiled his plan to "*place a floor under the income of every family with children in America*". In the late 1960s, there had been several Basic Income experiments in cities across America and in Canada. One unexpected result from the experiment in Seattle, saw the end of a national Basic Income policy before it even began. During the Seattle basic income experiment, there was a rise of 50 percent in divorce rates among the studied population. It is thought that mostly women in bad relationships, now having a certain financial security,

---

4. On this concern, I would recommend reading Bertrand Russel's 1935 essay *In Praise of Idleness*, which I feel addresses beautiful this concern.

decided to leave their spouses. For Nixon's conservative base, this collateral effect would have been unacceptable and so the project of a national Basic Income was scratched from the docket.

Potential mass poverty in the next couple decades still looms and regardless of it being a solution or not, UBI cannot be treated as all or nothing solution. To dismiss it forthright is foolish and to adopt it in one fell swoop is reckless. The only possibility is to trial it and learn from the results like Finland is doing.

Actually, Finland has put in place an innovative process for trialling complex policies before beginning the actual legislative process. Basic Income is one of the twenty experimental policies in the first run of this new political tool. This experimental process was designed with the help of the Finnish innovation consultancy *DemosHelsinki*[5], and though the current government is not trialling Basic Income for the reason of designing a new social security system[6], the experimental approach taken is I believe one that should inspire us all. Instead of continuing stale debates on unpredictable outcomes, this experimental approach enables both action, knowledge for future decisions, and maybe most basic of all greater education for citizens on policies.

---

5. See interview of Roope Mokka, Founder of DemosHelsinki

6. The Finnish Government wishes to see if Basic Income could be an incentive for people to accept short term or part-time jobs, following the philosophy that working more regardless of the nature of work is overall better for the economy and the country. A very industrial perspective and one which does not take into account the possibility of mass automation in the future. See the interviews of Timo A. Tanninen, Ministerial Counsellor for Finance, Vice Head of Unit for Planning and Development at the Finnish Ministry of Social Affairs and Health, and the interviews of Olli Kangas and Ville-Veikko Pulkka, respectively Head of Research and Basic Income Researcher at Kela.

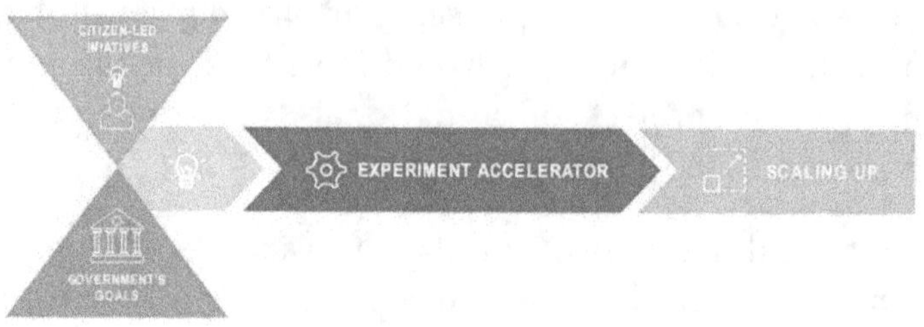

The basics of Finland's Policy Experimentation Process (DemosHelsinki)

Whether at an institutional level, like in Finland, or an individual[7] or organisational one, we should learn to develop our experimental capacity to trial new ideas. We have to learn to design experiments which both achieve results, while reducing failure and scaling risks, and from which we can learn for future action.

7.2. Design to Solve Multiple Issues

Famously, one of Google's mantras is "Don't be evil", but I prefer Taiwanese Member of Parliament, Jason Hsu's approach "create more value than you consume"[8]. With society having multiple drivers today, business models need to intrinsically solve multiple solutions and not just focus on revenue. Yes, a complicated challenge but one that some are rising to meet by designing business and organisational models which also address other societal issues, that try to "do more good" and not just no evil.

In Wellington, New Zealand, I interviewed Joshua Vial, one of the instigators of *Enspiral*, a new kind of

---

7. To see one example of an individual approach to life changes, I recommend you read Bill Burnett and Dave Evans *Designing your Life : Build a life that works for you,* and for leaders and managers interested in rethinking these questions in the context of their profession and organisation, I would direct you to Otto Sharmer's work on Theory U.

8. See Jason Hsu's interview on the study's website.

organisation, a cooperative of entrepreneurs. Joshua describes the development of this organisation in deceptively simple and unpretentious terms but you can see that much thought and effort has been put in designing such a structure[9].

"I realised that there were too few jobs which lined up with what people most wanted to work on, and the issues that matter. So, I thought that if I could help more people quit their job and become freelancers, and self-fund into change work, then we could get more people to work on issues that mattered [...].

[As an independent programmer,] I said yes to every contract that came my way, scrambled to find people and programmers. A lot of people I worked with would only do one or two contracts, but over time I kept selecting for aligned values and, some people hung around. When you're a freelancer you're often getting leads for work you can't do but when you have a whole bunch of friends you can pass them on to, it helps everyone. We became a big referral network.

We also started looking into decentralised organising and non-hierarchical structures, future organisational structures... We started a whole series of experimentations on how you do that in practice. By this stage, quite a few people were increasing their disposable time and money, and saw that commercial ventures were a good way to change the world. If you can create full-time jobs for people, where they are working on the stuff they really want to, then work becomes a mission. So, we gradually transitioned into social entrepreneurship and social ventures.

Over time, we shifted from being a cooperative of freelancers to a cooperative of entrepreneurs. That is pretty much the point where we are now.

[...]

---

9. For the full account, please read Joshua Vial's interview on the study's website.

The model I imagine [for the future of Enspiral] are hundreds of these entrepreneurial cooperatives helping one another in a peer to peer sort of way. Maybe they have roughly twenty or thirty businesses each, if one starts to get traction, the whole network swarms in and scales it with local money and local talent. If you think about Uber finding a model with definite traction, they raise funds though venture capital and then build a command-and-control hierarchical structure to scale this idea globally, which will mostly give the value away to the shareholders, a net loss for society. The value created will be less than the value paid. If instead, you utilised this web of existing two hundred coops, who all know one another and one of them comes up with an idea with traction, all the others can raise their own money, their own teams, and scale it out that way, with the core IP or brand treated as a common that everyone owns and stewards together for the benefit of all of them. This way would scale business globally very quickly with the value remaining in society.

Organic farmers sometimes say "I farm the soil not the plants". The work I'm very interested in is farming the ecosystem, helping to build these relationships, from which these ventures will grow. That is my main theory of change at the moment."

Obviously, such a model may struggle to scale, but *Enspiral* is trying to develop meaningful jobs and ventures while using its own organisational model to solve the inbuilt inequality of our current corporate finance model. Michel Bauwens, a Belgian economist specialised in Commons, also considers cooperatives such as *Enspiral,* as a way to solve part of our Global-Locals issue [10]

"I imagine using the Commons and in particular Digital

---

10. For a more comprehensive description of Michel Bauwen's theories, please read his interview on the study's website.

Commons, for the creation of new transnational structures, which would live next to existing inter-national structures. Karl Polanyi, in his book The Great Transformation, *talks about what he calls the "double movement". The History of capitalism moves back and forth between free market periods, which are phases of economic liberalisation, and regulatory periods, roughly changing every thirty years. Unfortunately today, this pendulum is broken. Capital is transnational but regulations are still decided at a State level, so popular revolts (either on Bernie Sanders' side or Donald Trump's side) are incapable of leading to market regulation. So, our economic system is broken.*

The solution I propose is that the ethical and generative coops and civic coalitions which create commons throughout the world, start being organised transnationally and trans-locally. This includes city coalitions such as the 40-city coalition to regulate Uber. This shows that this transnational regulatory movement is both top-down and bottom-up. The crisis in the Nation-State model is leading to the emergences of this new counter-power."

These examples show how to question the purpose of one's organisation and use its existence and structure to solve multiple issues in our societal model. To give a less radical illustration, while in Nairobi, I questioned Bob Collymore, the CEO of *Safaricom*, and the largest company in East Africa, on what his organisation's purpose was. His answer : "Transforming Lives" [11]. Bob Collymore was welcoming and very generous with his valuable time. Picture a gentle, bright and amazingly charismatic leader, and simply a very nice person when reading the following :

"What we mean by "Transforming Lives" can maybe be best explained through an illustration. Take a base station we set up in a place called Kapedo. It is an area subject to

---

11. For the whole answer, please read Bob Collymore's interview on the study's website.

intertribal clashes. This base station not only allows people to speak to one another, it allows them to call for help. This increases security. By putting a base station there, we also bring electricity to the area. By doing that, you now give people access to mobile health solutions, you allow children to be connected to the internet, you can bring mobile money and increase cash velocity. This is just an example, but we don't install base stations just to make revenue out of phone calls. When you look at our financials, you find that actually, less than 50% of our revenue is made by traditional voice calling. We start with the purpose, by wanting to change the situation.

Another example is putting a base station in Dadaab refugee camp [12] . Again, you build it there because you think you can transform the lives of people living there. All of which are somehow separated from their base. Now the result of doing that, is that Dadaab has become the first or second largest revenue earning "city" in the country. A lot of people go there and just look at ROI [13] but it isn't only about ROI."

Listening to Bob Collymore explain how this social proposition is placed "at the heart of the business, in every decision [Safaricom] makes", I felt elated and at the same time, sceptical. Why did I doubt this man's sincerity? He had given me no reason to in his manner or demeanour. The only reason I could think of was that I was suspicious of a person in a position of power saying such things. Affected by Lord Acton's philosophy that *"Power tends to corrupt [and] great men are almost always bad men."*, I was too quick to believe that CEOs of large corporations, the top 1%, are mostly selfish and only do good when we, the customers, NGOs, the government, make them accountable and keep them honest. Thinking of it further,

---

12. Dadaab Refugee Camp, in the Garissa region of Kenya, is the largest in the world with close to 500 000 refugees living there, mostly from Somalia.
13. Return On Investment

I realised that worldwide, though far from being in the top 1%, I am maybe in the top 10%, and if I believe in social good and helping others, why could it not be the case for this man? Though our system may try to keep some bad men in check, maybe it was also responsible for limiting some great men from doing more good. Indeed, Bob Collymore is responsible for the company's +4,000 employees' livelihood, and that responsibility may limit his otherwise more social goals.

The future will tell if Bob Collymore was being honest or just a great and charismatic communicator, but I prefer to believe that what he told me, and many other examples in companies around the world, is the beginning of a greater societal consciousness in corporations. The corporate world may not incentivise many actions beyond production and revenue growth but the people who work there are also members of society and are influenced by the same aspirations and dreams as the rest of us. Maybe my naivety will lead to disappointment – though having worked for some of the largest corporations in Europe both from within and as a consultant, I think I am quite objective when it comes to the corporate world – but scepticism would have a much greater cost : not allowing the possibility for change.

Some organisations, both old and new, are using their structures and influence to solve societal issues and correct the system's inherent flaws. This is how we should think for all our actions; how we can solve many problems simultaneously. It is possible and others are doing it.

7.3. Circumventing the System

Teresa Shook is a 60-year-old retired lawyer in Hawaii. Self-admittedly not very political, she nevertheless, like most of her fellow Americans – and many across the world – watched live the results of the November 8, 2016 Presidential Elections on television. Disappointed by the results, she posted on Facebook that she felt a pro-woman march was needed. A few dozen of her friends supported her and said they would attend, when she went to bed that night. The next morning 10,000 people had RSVPed but no official wanted to take over the organisation of the movement. So, Teresa Shook just did it herself. On January 21st, the movement she created saw a pink sea of 500,000 people march in Washington D.C. Globally, an estimated 4,400,000 people [14] took part in the Women's March [15].

Credentials, official positions and expertise undoubtedly help, no question about it, but today, legitimacy in many cases, comes from action. Traditional power structures are adapting to this reality. For example, while in Athens, I met with Christos Karras [16], who works on the digital platform *SynAthina*, the city's citizen initiative platform. There are currently over 250 active citizen groups on the site, all aiming in different ways, at increasing the quality of life within the Greek capital. Not only does the platform encourage and help citizens to take matters into their own hands, a growing number of civil servants from City Hall are using it to better understand the will of their citizens and connect directly with groups they can help, bypassing the usual hierarchical paths of communication within the city, like a modern-day Agora.

Digital tools have also enabled people to circumvent classical financial institutions through crowdfunding and

---

14. Figures by Jeremy Pressman, University of Connecticut, and Erica Chenoweth, University of Denver.

15. Actually, when considering the major Anti-Trump movements in the United States (*Swing Left, Indivisible, Daily Action*) they all emerged from people circumventing the established liberal structures. All three movements were started by individuals, not the big think tanks, advocacy groups or even the Democratic Party. This is a great example of how circumventing the system is generating a real, nation level movement

16. Please read Christos Karras' full interview on the study's website.

not only for business ventures, but in many other areas such as the arts (*PledgeMusic, Kickstarter* or *Indiegogo*) or scientific research (*Experiment* or *PetriDish*). With online classes, blogs, wikis, educative video channels (PBS IdeaChannel, *Vox*, etc.), knowledge on any topic is increasingly easily accessible. Access to skilled experts is not as difficult as you may think. There are platforms of freelancers (*Upwork, Toptal, Elance*) and my study is a good illustration of that as well. Out of the two-dozen amazing people I interviewed this year, which include CEOs of corporations, University Professors, Diplomats, Ministers, Members of Parliament, famous TEDsters, I knew none when I started out and I am not famous or was not backed by any institution to approach them. The internet also offers access to wide crowds of like-minded people to share your projects and ideas with.

What once was only possible to do by few or by large entities, is now democratised to many : creating global currencies (Bitcoin) or even creating States (see previous examples). This means that there is no reason (or excuse) to wait for the usual actors to solve issues if you believe something needs to be done. I am surprised actually, that there has not been yet a parallel tax system created anywhere in the world. If you were unhappy with the results of an election say, little would stop you from creating a voluntary crowdfunding site to enable people to finance the areas of State action discarded by the Government in power. Why wait several years for the next election, hoping somebody else solves the problem you wish to address ?

We are living in a time of great empowerment but also increased responsibility and potential guilt due to inaction. We should embrace this unprecedented ecosystem of meaningful action enabling. We should feel neither coerced or bullied into action, nor let apathy settle in because of all we could do. We should feel elated by the ability to circumvent existing systems and structures, take things into our hands, and follow a handful of causes we care about (whatever the size). If everyone did so, the world would be a much better place, by "creating more value than one consumes". Just take as an example, *Bye Bye Plastic Bags*, an international movement to ban plastic bags started by two young girls in Indonesia[17], which leads me to the next way we can improve our ability to succeed in this transitional time : Education

7.4. Learning How to Think, Not What to Know

John Hunter[18] speaks with the gentle humility of great teachers. There is a communicative calm and patience to the cadence of his sentences, which makes you feel like something important is being discussed and imparted to you. John seems completely focused on you, even when speaking with great modesty of his own work. It took all of a few seconds for me to want him as one of my teachers and regret no longer being a teenager for that to be a reality.

John is a Middle School teacher and the creator of the World Peace Game, a 2x2x2 meter turn-by-turn board game, where students as young as 9 years old, assemble in governments of fictitious and very different countries and solve fifty interlocking problems as complex as water resources, poverty, hunger, green-house gas emissions, while increasing wealth for every nation and ending the game with the World at peace. To achieve this wildly ambitious goal, the players can do whatever they want as long as they follow three rules : "*They have to be able to pay*

17. Students at the *Green School* in Bali, which I will discuss in the next section.
18. Please read John Hunter's full interview on the study's website.

for it, it has to make sense and they have to be able to deal with consequences (which, of course, they cannot see initially because they only play one step ahead at a time)". The Game has many small details which contribute to its genius, such as if you go to war with a neighbouring State, the children need to write a letter to the parents of the soon to be dead soldiers. I am being too terse, but the Game is absolutely brilliant and I feel it should be obligatory in educational curriculums around the world. However, after talking with its creator for an hour, he very kindly told me that I was missing the point of it.

I thought the World Peace Game was a great educational tool for children to learn complex problem solving, interpersonal skills, content on all these issues, responsibility, forecasting... there was so much learning there that I asked John on what his focus was. His answered really surprised me :

"There is such a high signal to noise ratio and so much information today, on what is proper, what is right, what is best, what should be done... that I try to avoid giving my own opinion on that. To do so only leads to people making decisions based on what feels good or how they feel about you, and that just adds to the difficulty of choosing. I would just be adding to the noise, in a sense. I should contextualise my answer before giving it, here.

I believe the universal thing that we can all agree upon is introspection : Know Thy Self. From that point, you may gain a lever to move the world, so to speak. Immediately, if you truly, regularly, minutely examine and come to know yourself, you start seeing interdependency, and then compassion arises. Caring for others and self-knowledge are the primary, universal, overarching and deepest skills for me."

The educational model we inherited from the industrial era follows similar rules to industrial manufacturing.

Students are products along a multi-year assembly line where they gradually gain knowledge and undergo regular quality control, called exams. It is a mass and standardised approach to teaching, which once again, improved the world dramatically. However, faced with today's complex choices, knowing who we are and finding the universal within us are two basic skills that are necessary and hardly compatible with the standardised approach. Thankfully, a lot of education systems around the world are transitioning, but the imprint of the industrial heritage is still very visible everywhere.

Though, I agreed with those values, I asked John about content, because schools should still impart knowledge to anchor our thinking into reality. John agreed that content was important but not as straightforward a question as maybe it once was :

"It is important when imparting knowledge to children, to also show them the relativity of that knowledge.

To give you an example. A few years ago, I taught a class on how to use the internet. I asked the children to visit a website dedicated to the Pacific North West Tree Octopus, a rare and endangered species. The kids loved it and the website had all kinds of knowledge and facts, it looked very professional. Of course, all the information was fictional, there is no such animal. That example was used to show that we need to see beyond presentation, to show students that they must discern what's true. Looking at mainly by who is saying it and how it is being said, is not enough.

Our big problem is to know what actually is. Today there are so many people competing to tell you what "is". The issue I have found with students in the last few years is that because of this overabundance of information, their creativity has been stifled. Children today, seem to not even need an imagination really. Imagination has been pre-packaged for them 24/7 so as to keep them engaged.

Recently, I gave an exercise in creative writing to 3rd graders – they just love creative writing. However, I told them they could write about anything but; this time there couldn't be any monster, any pets or any explosions -no one gets killed or hurt – or any aliens. They stopped abruptly and one boy asked incredulously : "Well, what are we going to write about, then ? What's left ?!" If you knock down the convention – and that is my job as a teacher, to wipe out conventional thinking to some degree – the kids struggle but it is important for them to do so. You need to take away what they think is so that they can discover what actually is in their own lives."

It is true that with all the screens around us, adults and children alike, are no longer bored, though it is out of boredom that creativity arises. With so many issues to solve, creativity is something that we need to protect and encourage. So, how different should we make school in the 21st century to educate the next few generations ? Maybe not so different after all, was Leslie Medema's answer, the Principal of the *Green School* in Bali [19].

The *Green School* is one of the most progressive schools in the world. The reason for this success is focus on three aspects of education : the learning program, of course, but also two others which are most often overlooked in traditional institutions : the learning environment and the learning community. For both these last aspects, the *Green School* is uniquely privileged in a way not easily replicable. Students learn in a lush, beautiful hamlet of magical wall-less huts built completely out of bamboo which feels out of the pages of a crossover adventure between *Harry Potter* and the *Swiss Family Robinson*. As for the learning community, besides incredibly dedicated and privileged parents, the Green School benefits from visits

---

19. Please read Leslie Medema's full interview on the study's website.

from some of the greatest minds of our time, the likes of Ban-Ki Moon or Jane Goodall. Obviously, duplicating such a model worldwide would be nigh-impossible but the way the Green School thinks about their learning program could easily inspire other schools. This is how Leslie Medema describes their teaching philosophy :

"A lot of our curriculum isn't any different to many other schools. We have maths classes, history classes, English classes, etc. The difference comes from how we structure it.

For example, a Grade 10 student will have a required history course that runs all year long. That history course will have both factual knowledge components as well as historical analysis skills. But after that, the students can choose all kinds of history courses and they change their classes every six weeks. They can choose to go in greater depth or explore other themes.

Students will also have a certain amount of math to learn. We may give it a funky name, we try to make it fun for them, but in reality, they are doing "Algebra 1" with a twist. We try to make it engaging, to bring in the environment, to bring in real-world examples. We have a bio bus program, where we transform cooking oil into bio fuel to run our school buses on. At the moment, a lot of our chemistry and mathematics curriculum is taught through that program. Students in primary school learn exponents by taking out loans from the student bank we have, so they can buy chickens, so that they can have a chicken coop; eventually they will repay the loan with the eggs that are laid. We try to apply the teaching to real-world examples as much as we can, but if we can't, we will do problem sets, and that is also fine. We haven't thrown out by any stretch, all the curriculum babies with all the bath waters, because brilliant people around the world have created that and with good reason. We really believe in multiplication tables, which throws people off sometimes (laugh), but if we can do that by building a garden for example, then we will do it that way.

Over the course of six years, we have studied seven of the world's best curriculums and built our own, based on core principles and skills. You then have some proficiency classes, which are just about that, but the majority of classes will be thematic and integrated. If you can include a project in the course, then that's the key. A lot of curriculum uses inquiry-based skills as well. "

I asked Leslie to illustrate what one of these projects could be and she described to me one of the projects she had created and taught.

"I taught a class for a couple years on religions. I was just tasked with teaching students the very basics of several different faiths. We [the teaching team] also had this skill that we wanted them to learn which was business writing : synthesizing a lot of information and putting an argument to your boss about what needs to be done. I had these two things and we found the idea of studying the pig (because we have pigs at the school), as a way for all of us (the students and myself) to learn about something together. The pig is a fascinating animal to study in regards to faith. We would also look at the pig in literature and read anything from Charlotte's Web to Animal Farm. We looked at pigs in language : you have capitalist pigs and communist pigs, pigs can mean cops, and we just went on and on and on.

We looked at the environmental impact of the animal and it all ended with the students researching slaughtering methods, to make sure the animals were well treated but also economically viable for the farmers. So, the students read about Temple Grandin and her work and wrote memos to slaughtering facilities that weren't using best practices, best practice defined as a method that was best for the animal, the meat (and hence the sale of the meat), the environment, and the society (appeases animal rights activists).

We also went to a slaughter house and the concept was that "you didn't have to go but if you ate meat, you should". And in Indonesia it's fascinating because they pray for every animal before killing it but it is still a difficult scene to watch. At this point, the students know all about pigs, have been holding them, know that our eyes are the same, that we can have heart valve transplants from them, etc."

When listening to Leslie or John, compared to friends of mine in the *Education Nationale* in France, what struck me was that to help students find out who they were, it seemed important for teachers to express their own individuality in how they taught. The standardisation of our classical educative systems does not only apply to students but also teachers....and university professors.

Jonathan Dawson is a Professor of Economics and Director of the Economics of Transition Masters at Schumacher College in Devon. Though with older students, his attitude to teaching resembles much that of John's and Leslie's : *"I see my role as facilitating the discourse of the students and helping their ideas emerge, adapting myself to what they wish to discover".* Jonathan has questioned not only the content of Economics degrees but also mostly how content is taught. He has found that there were three educational principles of teaching that we take for granted but are questionable if not wholly wrong :

— *"The role of the teacher is transmissive"* : Knowledge in the classroom in traditionally unidirectional, from the teacher to the pupils. It negates the possibility of students teaching one another and even more, teachers learning from their students.

— *"Transmission is solely done using the intellect"* : The general thinking is that we only learn with our rational mind. Neuroscience is disproving that. Anyone having done a highly technical sport such as golf, rowing, rugby, gymnastics, or learned an instrument will know that your body needs to learn movements that by simply thinking you cannot achieve. As Jonathan explains, *"some researchers believe we only learn through the body and then, make sense of it with our minds. Students in the Economics of Transition Master, and in general at Schumacher College, are invited to be the new economy not to only study it"* [20].

— *"Education is an individual and not a group process"* : Learning is thought to occur individually within one's own mind, which seems actually not to be completely true. *"More broadly speaking and because of the institute's history, we are strongly influenced by Mindfulness and oriental tradition. This is why, group learning is also important within the College (peer assessment, teacher assessment...). Psychologists have shown that business students are "meaner" that other students because of what they learn (the world is cutthroat, competition, etc.). The type of community learning that happens here helps with that."*

Clearly, much can be done in our education system to prepare us and future generations for this new page of decision-making in Human History. Leslie summed up beautifully how she saw the educative system of the 21st century.

"I believe there is a set of classic knowledge, a way of

---

20. I asked Jonathan to elaborate on this point : *"This realisation occurred to me about 15 years ago. I noticed that when lecturing on problems such as global warming, or revenue inequality, or global poverty, students went straight into problem-solving mode. There was no emotional reaction to these problems, which I did not feel was normal. At the end of the class, it was as if nothing had happened during the two-hour discussing these issues. The students came out as they came in. Not much learning had happened and no change had occurred, at least, no behavioural change.So, I decided to try and use theatre in the classroom. I asked the students to group themselves into "continents" and each group to walk in a circle : the number of students per continent proportional to the continent's population relative to the world, the diameter of the circle proportional to the continent's average wealth per capita. The students in the "North America" circle said afterwards that they felt a little lonely looking all that was going on in the "African" circle for example and saw the feeling of community that large number of people in close proximity generated. That is learning that would not have happened in a classroom with only facts, figures and theory."*

thinking that needs to be acquired over time as well.

It is also about understanding the concept that you have a responsibility to make a positive difference within your community. It can be small [...] but you need to be productive, be healthy and you need to do something for others. [...] You need to leave this school with that level of responsibility.

For me the 21st and 22nd centuries are about bringing back that concept that you owe something to your community, to put back more than you take out. It can be very simple though. You do not want to put the huge responsibility of changing the world on the shoulders of kids. You don't need to, but if everyone acted in this way, we wouldn't need to in the first place. And I think it is possible. Kids are amazing, they love to help, they want to give back. It is just instilling this idea instead of telling them that they need to get the best grade on this test, to do this, to do that to become a successful person."

7.5. Seizing the Opportunity of Populism

Though educating new generations to improve their ability to decide in our extremely complex world is necessary, I have always disliked the idea of pushing back the responsibility of change on future generations. By definition, death is the cessation of all functions that sustain an organism. I think of society as an organism and action of its members is the price to pay to be part of a healthy society. This does not necessarily mean going forward, it can mean going in another direction, even moving backwards, but it does mean moving. We should act like adults and not hope that our children or grandchildren be better and do more than ourselves are willing to do today. Leading by example is I believe the best way to ensure an engaged progeny. Furthermore, to expect only part of society to act, implies depriving ourselves of the richness of other perspectives.

In 2014, a student protest in Taiwan became a national movement of change. The *Sunflower Movement* – though much more successful than its Hong Kong contemporary counterpart, the *Umbrella Movement*[21] – was for some reason, much less covered in Western Media. Initially opposing the adoption of a Trade Agreement with Mainland China, the opposition movement – which at one point occupied the Taiwanese Legislature for two weeks – lead to the ruling party's replacement after nearly seven decades of Kuomintang presidential dominance, in the May 2016 elections.

Though maybe the most obvious, the change of government is not to me the most interesting aspect of the Sunflower Movement. The Movement lead to leaps in the advancement of *civictech*, or technology-aided democracy. As Liz Barry recounts in her first-hand account[22] of the movement, this is what she saw in the streets of Taipei during 2014 :

"Groups of strangers armed with post-it notes intensely deliberated policy points and DIY antenna-wielding tech crews broadcast those street deliberations to millions. Amidst the hand-painted banners, giant puppets, and stacked bedrolls were weather-proofed racks of servers, broadcast equipment, and dishes powered by thick electrical cables running out of the open windows of the occupied legislative building. [...]

In late April 2014, after the Sunflower Movement had ended, the same "deliberation in the street" (dstreet) team held another round of public deliberations on nuclear energy,

---

21. I also travelled to Hong Kong and to understand the differences between these two movements, I recommend you read Kin-man Chan's and Emily Lau's interviews on the study's website.

22. *vTaiwan : Public Participation Methods on the Cyberpunk Frontier of Democracy*, Liz Barry, August 11 2016

and yet another set on constitutional reform.

[...] Ever since the Sunflower Movement, members of the open source community and Taiwan's government had been collaboratively developing a novel, effective conglomeration of civic technologies, government commitments, and mass media dedicated to the public conversation needs of a nation's democratic process. They call it vTaiwan"

vTaiwan emerged in December 2014, when then-Minister Tsai Ing-Wen asked g0v.tw, one of Taiwan's main digital activist communities if they *"Could create a platform for rational discussion and deliberation of policy issues that the entire nation could participate in ?"*. In return, she promised that the Government would be bound by the popular consent expressed on the platform during its legislative process.

When Tsai Ing-Wen became President in 2016, she continued to embrace the used of civictech, including by appointing Audrey Tang, a digital *hack-tivist* from g0v.tw and as self-taught programming prodigy, as Digital Minister [23]. *vTaiwan* is a fast-moving process thanks to its many contributors but, I wish to give one brief example of what it allows.

Pol.is is one of the many tools that make up *vTaiwan*. This online survey tool allows user to "agree," "disagree," or "pass" in response to statements other users have given. The user can then also add a statement describing their own opinion on the issue, which in turn, will be proposed to other users for them to take position. Users are automatically grouped in real time following their position. This process continues until the position of the population is refined and clear on the given topic. This consensus-building method successfully help with the policy adopted by the Government concerning the

---

23. Please read Audrey Tang's full interview on the study's website

entrance of Uber on the island and help find in under six months, a solution to a six-year stalemate concerning online alcohol sales.

Philosophers of the Enlightenment mostly discarded the possibility of Direct Democracy because of their practical inability to scale such a system. They could not foresee that two centuries later, we would have technology that could maybe start to make this model feasible. As I have already mentioned, there are many pitfalls in developing a more direct model of democracy, but broader citizen implication seems not only possible, but the Taiwanese experiments seem to show that it could solve some complex issues our current model is struggling with. Furthermore, broader understanding from citizens on the choices our societies face can only increase hope in successfully navigating this Era of Transition.

I have used the term "citizen" several times in this essay, but it is maybe worth questioning its use briefly. As Raf Manji, a former London financier and now member of the Christchurch City Council in New Zealand, argues. We may have gradually reverted to being subjects and no longer citizens. As he describes, *"subjects are passive, are victims, are represented, are served, and are beneficiaries. They are a consumer. It is easy"*. On the other hand, *"citizens are active, responsible, creative, are agents and recipients. They are participant. It is difficult."* However, as he points out as well society is not meant to be easy. As I have illustrated when underlining the difference in referenda numbers between Great Britain and Switzerland, most of us only engage periodically with the running of our society and that is why we are disengaged. Raj Manji calls for a new Social Contract to be written, one to make us citizens again. He is not the only one.

In a time of growing populism, it may be surprising

to think optimistically about the future of democracy but it is in Taipei, during this time of civictech boom, that I met with Stéphane Corcuff, the current Director of the French Center for the Study of Contemporary China (CEFC) and an expert on political regimes both in Europe and in the "Chinese World" [24] who convinced me that nationalism and populism may offer us a much more exciting alternative :

"[I believe] Europe might have never been democratic yet, not to mention in some other parts of the world, where the culture of public debate is not as important as in Europe.

Various democratic models that exist are procedural democracies, ensuring the fairness of selection of candidates to power and of the elections, the definition of the electorate, how powers are organized and limited by responsibilities and recall, how to implement a due process of law and the regular extension of civil and human rights etc. Yet, unfortunately, democracies stopped short of educating all citizens beyond writing, counting, plus a professional training, and it is all but normal that it is hard for all to be able to think and decide about complex national issues : there are many, they are urgent, they are terribly technical, their moral or value-based stakes are considerable. We always quote the education project of the Third Republic in France, yet it was already dealing with immensely complex issues (colonialism, the separation between the Church-State, the 20s economic and social crises ...) which a normal citizen cannot understand easily. However, we have to vote, and we mandate our representatives, whom we all know are extremely busy, to understand such issues and make the right decisions for us. How we can simply trust them is one issue and how we can blame them all the time, while it is actually so comfortable to just not to do the job by ourselves, is another one.

---

24. Mainland China, Hong Kong, Taipei

We could recognize that we live in procedural democracies, that would be honest, and we'd go further deepening our democratic systems. But most of the time, we don't, and therefore, we fail to face the real problems of democracies. I do not believe the corruption of politicians is the most important factor that produces low voting rates, I believe it is the unsubstantiated power attached to the ballot. This paves the way for other forms of mobilization, which are detrimental to the democratic polity.

Populism, often presented as being exemplified by the Brexit, the election of Trump, the rise of right-wing parties (but rarely presented as equally exemplified by leftist populism) may not herald the end of democracies, and on the contrary, may announce, if we seize this opportunity of democratic crisis, the beginning of a new phase of democracy, with the help of a better civic education and the new technologies of information and communication, a phase in which public debates will be returned to citizens who will question experts and not need to go through representatives for each issue. But the challenge is immense, as we could also see a process of fragmentation of political decisions, made by and based on emotions, which the NTICs are also well-known to channel."

It may be easier today to create parallel systems than going through existing representative channels, and this even may be a good way to improve our societal mechanics. However, that does not mean that we should completely abandon our historical organisations altogether. After centuries of gradual evolution, our political regimes have become highly sophisticated and balanced if still far from perfect. The luxury of the past half-century in the West has allowed us to grow somewhat complacent of democracy, but the predictable authoritarian backlash of such passive contentment may give us the momentum we require, for not only reverting to the state of affairs we have grown accustomed to, but even progress further on the path of democratisation.

7.6. Embracing community

Bill McKibben wrote *The End of Nature* in 1989, considered by many the first book for a general audience on climate change and founded *350.org* in 2007. The slightly esoterically named[25] NGO is today one of the leading organisations in the fight against climate change. In a recent online article[26], McKibben writes that the most common question people ask him has encouragingly remained the same over the years : "How can I help?". However, his answer has changed.

From recommending individual actions to reduce one's carbon footprint, McKibben has gradually asked people to reconsider their initial question and ask not "What can I do?", but "What can **we** do?". As he puts it, *"The most important thing an individual can do is not be an individual because changing oneself doesn't change the group. Community is not just the sum of the individualities that make it up"*[27].

Time and time again during these months of study, I have been confronted with the feeling of *Zeitgeist*, the spirit of the age. Like convergent evolution, similar ideas seemed to appear in disconnected situations and faraway places. Quite possibly links exist and were simply too

---

25. 350.org takes its name from NASA climate scientist James Hansen's contention that "if humanity wishes to preserve a planet similar to that on which civilization developed and to which life on Earth is adapted, paleoclimate evidence and ongoing climate change suggest that CO2 will need to be reduced from its current 385 ppm to at most 350 ppm, but likely less than that". This quote comes from James Hansen's book *Where should humanity aim?* published in 2008. Since then the amount of CO2 in the atmosphere has continued to increase. In March 2017, at the time of writing, the planetary average was of 407,05ppm, and climbing.

26. *The Question I Get Asked the Most*, Bill McKibben – EcoWatch, October 14[th,] 2016

27. Rousseau's insights in *Du Contrat Social* hard at work once more.

complex for me to grasp, or as likely, I unwittingly may have been that link myself hit by lasting and multiple bouts of Baader-Meinhof syndrome [28]. However, the more I travel, the more it feels to me that consciousness permeates our global society, one which seems to act somewhat independently from the conscious individuals who populate it. As I have mentioned before, we still have much to discover about community dynamics and I have no scientific backing for this notion, but I admit being partial to this image of communities as conscious organisms made up of other individual organisms. This is not by any means unique in nature.

Indeed, you may be surprised to learn that there are 10 times more bacterial cells in your body than human cells [29]. Furthermore, without all these organisms you would die, and without your own cells, so would these bacterial colonies. Those "alien" cells – though devoid of consciousness as far as we know – still follow some basic rules to perpetuate their species and survive, as do our own human cells. Together they make up a human body, with its own consciousness and governing dynamics.

Though we might not yet understand the decision processes, we know that groups and communities act differently to individuals, even to the individuals who make up these communities. Furthermore, as the realisation slowly dawns that the solutions to our global issues are hindered by our lack of global institutions or planetary decision-making tools, this notion of

---

28. The proper name of this syndrome is "Frequency Illusion", coined in 2006 by Stanford linguistics professor Arnold Zwicky, this syndrome is the phenomenon wherein a concept or thing you just found out about suddenly seems to crop up everywhere. The story behind the "Baader-Meinhof phenomenon" name dates back to 1994, when on the St. Paul *Pioneer Press'* online discussion board, someone invented it after hearing the name of the German terrorist group twice in the same day.

29. This is according to Carolyn Bohach, a microbiologist at the University of Idaho. For those having difficulty believing such a thing, remember that bacterial cells are far smaller than most human cells.

community – in particular global community – seems to be making some headway. The predictable failure of nationalist movements to solve these issues will, in time, I believe, force us all to address these issues together. I share Gaspard Koenig's wish that *"these populist movements we are witnessing, in France with the Front National, in Britain with Brexit, and in the U.S. with Trump, are [but] the death rattle of this past society"*[30].

However, some have already started to tackle this complex issue of community. For example, you will have noticed in reading their interviews that the teachers I have presented to you are all sowing the seeds of community building within their classrooms, so that this notion feels more familiar to the next generation. And at the opposite scale, in February 2017, Mark Zuckerberg published his Manifesto[31] on his ambitions for the world's largest social network, which at the time of writing counted over 2 billion members. His goal is nothing short of making *Facebook* the main tool for this communal and global discourse. In his words : *"Facebook stands for bringing us closer together and building a global community"*[32]. Yet it is in Kibera, Kenya, that I saw first-hand how useful community tools could be at addressing complex systemic issues, and in Kenya, no issue is more complex or systemic than that of corruption.

A poster child for the *Africa Rising* narrative, Ruth Mwangi is a Director at *Grassroots Economics*, a non-profit which creates and operates local currencies for low-income communities in Kenya. Though there is nothing radically new about local currencies, in Kibera, the *Lindi-Pesa* not

---

30. See Gaspard Koenig's interview on the study's website.

31. *Building Global Community*, posted on Facebook on February 16th 2017

32. I highly recommend reading Yuval Noah Harari's answer to Mark Zuckerberg's Manifesto, published in the *Financial Times* on March 25, 2017, which points out the potential struggles *Facebook* may face in achieving this ambitious goal, given its current business model. However, such ambition should be encouraged.

only addresses the classic issues of economic stabilisation, but as Ruth explains : *"Another important advantage is the increased trust within the community. This is particularly important in a country with rampant corruption"* [33].

To try and comprehend the extent and complexity of corruption in a place like Kibera, I will let Hital Muraj, another brilliant Kenyan Woman working in Kibera, illustrate ever so briefly the situation [34] :

"Corruption is rampant [...]. Take Kibera for example. There is such a huge amount of aid being given there but there hasn't been any real change for years. It is actually getting worse because the mindset of people there is becoming used to and dependent on the system of aid put in place. I find there is very little courage in people to fight back.

[...]

I'll give you an example. I wanted to create a youth centre in Kibera and I looked for a space for four years. One day, I learned that a world-famous celebrity had given $1M to create a talent hub, which from what I heard, wasn't used much. I went in search of this place to see if it could house my programs. The building didn't exist. I stood in the spot where it was supposed to be, where the celebrity had been during an inauguration ceremony and there was nothing there. After that, I started getting death threats because I was digging for information. I have been mugged at gun point before and I know it is for similar reasons."

Ruth echoes Hital's analysis and shows the difference between aid and a community-building tool such as a local currency :

"There are more than 600 NGOs [35] *working [in Kibera] and*

---

33. See Ruth Mwangi's interview on the study's website.

34. See Hital Muraj's interview on the study's website.

35. Some estimate that there is one NGO for every 11 residents in Kibera slum. So even taking the lowest population estimate of the 'recorded' population of 170'070, that is over 15'000 NGOs.

hundreds of millions of dollars have been used to improve the status of this slum. The slum still stands and I have real trouble seeing any major difference over the last 10 years. It is like a certain balance has been struck between the poor, the aid and the NGOs. People on both sides become dependent on the system. We, [Grassroots Economics] do not want to become institutional. We want to help and then leave. [...] The local currency is made to disappear"

[...]

People in Kenya do not trust one another. They trust foreigners more or members of a given small community such as the Somalian Diaspora or the Indian Community, who are known to be very good businessmen and women. In Nairobi, one of the areas with the highest amounts of businesses is Eastleigh, we call it Small Mogadishu. Other Kenyans own similar businesses to the ones there but we prefer to go to Eastleigh because we trust them more than fellow Kenyans.

To build trust, we need to start at a community level, like we do with the local currencies, where people from different tribes learn to make small loans to each other and learn that the other pays it back, and so forth."

With digital tools, these communities need not be only geographically local and thus can be a true solution to the nationally institutionalised corruption in Kenya as Ruth explains :

"[Grassroots Economics plans] to bring rural areas into the mix so that the businesses using our local currencies can source produce directly from the farmers thus making the community more sustainable. We also want to create cooperatives to strengthen the whole enterprise and digitalise the currency, use M-Pesa[36] for example and create a "local" digital currency".

---

36. M-Pesa (M for mobile, *pesa* is Swahili for money) is a mobile phone-based money transfer, financing and microfinancing service, launched in 2007 by Safaricom.

Ruth's and Hital's inspiring work showed me the importance of considering community specifically in my study. However, it is in the city of Christchurch in New Zealand, at the bottom of our terrestrial globe, that I met one of the most cutting-edge community enablers on my journey, an architect who has decided to completely change the way we build our cities. Audaciously, she wants to build cities for people and communities.

On Tuesday February 22nd 2011, during lunchtime, the city of Christchurch was hit by a strong and very shallow earthquake. Six months prior, a stronger but deeper tectonic plate shift had already weakened many buildings in the city. Though this second earthquake only lasted 10 seconds, it caused the death of 181 people and destroyed a huge part of the buildings in what was then New Zealand's second most inhabited city. Of the 3000 buildings surveyed in the city centre after the disaster, 1250 of them were deemed unfixable and were torn down. Over 10,000 houses met the same faith in the city's suburbs. It is in this rubble that Camia Young, a successful American architect, saw an opportunity to give new life to this city and experiment her ideas about the community.

Camia has an impressive portfolio of work in some of the most renowned architecture firms in the world both in the United States and in Europe. Not alone in this realisation, she sees in our cities the urban vestiges of our industrial past. We built and still build cities mainly to transport goods. Urbanist design ways to bring people to areas of transformation, acquisition, or enjoyment of these goods, and many ways to transport these goods into, out of, and within cities. Our towns are mostly built for objects, not people. However, in many developed nations, manufacturing no longer plays the role it once did. To Camia and others, it no longer makes sense to build our cities following those obsolete rules. Instead, she proposes to redefine urbanism to favour the building of healthy communities. But one does one practically go about such an ambitious goal?

Exemplifying the experimental attitude I wrote about previously, Camia invested a sizeable amount of her savings into the creation of *OHU*[37], a foundation set up to create in a few months, the framework of this new type of urbanism. For instance, law historically enables us to protect our property from others, not to share it with them. Within *OHU*, a taskforce of lawyers is working on the legal frameworks which would enable such communal property. A similar task group is working on the financial structures to hold and take care of these community buildings. Yet another group is teaching inhabitants of the city to become better community builders, or as Camia calls them, Community Weavers. Camia plans to apply *OHU*'s methodologies to a portfolio of projects she has already started constituting around Christchurch, and to share the results so that other cities worldwide can benefit from her experimentation. Communities may have a certain will but it is with the work of people like Camia, that they will have agency and be able to mould the physical world around us.

All I have written up to this section, only concerned the individual, but group dynamics are different than just a weighted expression of the individualities within it. It is another level of complexity and one with which we need to compose moving forward. It is a level of thought, of consciousness, and of agency we have little experience of in the West, a culture that exacerbates the self. However, to address the issues of our time, it is imperative we act as individuals but also as members of a community or several communities. The most forward-thinking of us have not

---

37. Ohu means "communal work group" in Maori.

only adopted this acumen but are building tools for these communities to act and take part constructively in our future.

CONCLUSION

It may be a platitude, but the future is what we make of it. Whatever we may think, we are never passive, and ironically inaction is also a choice with its own consequences. The fact is that we have more than enough good reasons to actively change our society. Both the survival of *the* species [1] and our overall quality of life invite us to act. Maybe it even compels us, but that would negate the point I am trying to make : only we can choose to act. The simple reality that we are in a position to question the fundamental values of society may feel unsettling, but when trying to move, *unsettling* is exactly what we want. The only thing holding us back is our own uncertainty about the future.

Faced with such complexity, we sometimes feel tired before even trying. Where does one start? The framing of such a question is demoralising. One does not plan climbing a mountain by focussing on the cold, blizzard-washed summit and an empty backpack to fill. You need to focus on how it would feel to reach the summit and tell your friends about it over a good bottle of wine, around the fire place. This gives you enough energy to at least put the first pair of socks in the bag. Without utopias and positive narratives, it is hard to step into the unknown. We need excitement and hope for the future. We need to allow our optimism to carry us into the future we desire and not let the burden of our past weigh us down where we currently stand.

---

1. And many other species on earth.

We also have to change our perspective with regard to change. It is no longer simply about forcing the world and reality to comply with our ambitions and needs. We simply do not have the necessary stamina to continually approach problems piecemeal. We must abandon our puerile hubris and adapt to the world as much as we are adapting it to us. We should also embrace experimentation. If we try a new direction, knowing that it is an attempt, we can always change the path or backtrack if need be. We will advance faster this way, than planning an entire journey without adequate knowledge of a moving terrain.

Jonathan Dawson, at Schumacher College, encourages his students to think as "*Historians of the near future*". The way I understand the expression, is that we should take a step back and look at ourselves and our decisions from the perspective of a historian studying this period in time. What would you like the historian to report? If you create a narrative that excites you, that is probably what you should actually be doing.

The following narrative is quite personal and like any utopia, it is also laughably unrealistic, but so would a Europe at peace or men on the Moon have been to past generations. The purpose is not to convince you of my position, but rather to encourage you to undertake this exercise for yourself. The point is that we all need to come to our own conclusions and then work individually and collectively to make them a reality.

The following is part of the narrative that excites me about the future and which I wish to help write into future history books:

Around 2000 A.D. – at the beginning of what we call today the Helikian Era[2] - humanity came close to extinction. Though maybe surprising to us today, many were voluntarily

---

2. From hélikia (ἡλικία) in Greek, meaning maturity.

oblivious to the ostensible proof of the unsustainable nature of their global societal organisations. This proof was regularly shown in a variety of formats by the scientific community and relayed by the mass media. This highly documented time – thanks to the first version of the internet – is a great reminder to us today – facing the difficulties we know – that change is possible. Though we may today feel overwhelmed, our past generations felt similarly. They were tempted, as we are today, to deny what we need to do, but they instead found the courage to actively change society. We will always be indebted to them, as we all still are indebted to the Cold War generations for having had the wisdom not to end Humanity in a thermo-nuclear conflict.

Before today's more stable demographics, the exponential growth of the industrial era brought the human population up to 11 billion individuals in the mid-21st century. A majority lived in the most basic of conditions. The successful management of population growth and subsequent de-growth, the increase in efficiency of resource management and the increase in quality of life are really the crowning achievements of the Helikian generations. Following what at the time would have been called an international grass-roots movement, richer global citizens realised that it was in their interest to hasten the development of the so-called "developing nations". Many names were given to this movement, but we popularly refer to it today as "Selfish Sharing". This capital transfer was achieved through massive crowdfunding efforts for the education of women and universal access to basic needs (clean water, food, clean energy, education, housing). This hastened and finished demographic transition in all countries. Their successful management of the transition is the reason why we are here today. However, other transformations during that time explain the nature of our contemporary society.

Along with climate change, global inequality was the cause of many security issues and conflicts worldwide. Though few state-on-state wars took place, long drawn-out local conflicts and acts of global terrorism – sometimes organised by non-geographically local groups – created the perception of insecure times. Though in reality much safer than past centuries, this led to populist and isolationist movements for a time which slowed the transition. However, this reactionary movement is considered today, as one of the main drivers for the active involvement of many in the post-industrial transition, in effect a catalyst for change.

Inequality started to be discussed within nation-states as early as 2015, but it took another ten years, before humanity started to systematically address it on a global scale – having by that stage accepted the planetary nature of their society. First through grass-roots movements like the ones mentioned previously and then through institutional channels. That slow realisation concludes what we consider today the process of globalisation, which most agree started with the First World War. Though such a name may imply a realisation of the global nature of society, most people up to the mid-21st century still felt part of one nation before thinking of themselves as part of a global community, surprising as that may be.

This latency was in part due to the time required for the educational change-over to take effect. The so-called "Classroom Revolution", which took place during the second quarter of the 21st century, is thought to have been one of the great catalysts for the sustained change over the three key generations of the Helikian Era. Seen as a continuation of the industrial era's successful focus on giving all children a basic and standard set of skills and knowledge, the "Classroom Revolution" concentrated on teaching children to think critically and learn how to learn. This more customised approach to education gave children and then adults, greater adaptive capabilities, enabling individuals and communities to become more resilient.

The pace of change, technological development and new information having continued its exponential rise since the mid-19th century, this growing adaptive ability allowed humanity to successfully face a more fluid society. The Industrial Era is considered today the last "stable state" in History. The "Classroom Revolution" is seen by many to be the reason why we have been able to face constant societal flux since then. It also gave those generations a better understanding of complexity and of Humanity as being part of a larger planetary ecosystem.

Though difficult to believe today, most people in democracies at the beginning of the 21st century, limited their roles as citizens to voting and begrudgingly paying their taxes. With developments in information technology and the crisis in the representative model of government, the first half of the 21st century saw a great increase in voluntary networked structures, parallel to public and private institutions. This – along with the increasing realisation of globalisation – opened the debate on values in society, which over time, led to the creation of movements for the reallocation of wealth across geographies and borders. This in turn, led to an easier adoption of laws and international treaties, gradually creating the global supranational democratic power structure we know today, based on clearer checks and balances between the public sphere, private organisations and networked citizen movements.

An increase in ethical concerns over technological development laid the philosophical groundwork for the relatively progressive and successful adoption of A.I. and work automation. This visionary preparation and public debate, allowed the continuation of scientific and technological development, without too high a social cost. The early Helikian Era is today considered along with Antiquity, the Confucian Revolution and the Enlightenment as a fundamental age of philosophical progress.

This philosophical movement was also the genesis of a revised financial and economic system that was created to adapt to the manufacturing and service automation of the time. The private sector also grew in societal responsibility by transforming its relatively simplistic predatory nature into the more social structures present today. It may seem absurd but there was a time when the sole concern of organisations was infinite growth.

Finally, and more profoundly, a growing acknowledgment of community and not only individualism is arguably one of the least obvious but main characteristics of the Helikian Era. With gradual discoveries in neurosciences and societal dynamics, humanity started to better understand the reciprocal influences of community and the individual. These new discoveries led to more reforms in education, media, architecture and urbanism, and decision processes of all kinds, so that all parts of society benefited by the advantages offered by group dynamics.

All these changes may seem obvious to us today, but they required a global shift in mindsets unprecedented up to that point. Hindsight being 20/20, we feel that these changes make sense and had we been in their shoes we would have done it sooner, but if we are honest, the Helikian Era was a time of huge courage and responsibility and it is not so sure we would have fared so well.

That is my narrative, what is yours?

ACKNOWLEDGEMENT

Many contributed to this study, in fact too many to name them all. As I am mortified at the idea of forgetting someone, I will avoid naming individuals for the most part, but please know that, if at any point we talked in the last two years about virtually anything, I thank you for your help. You will have contributed in some specific way to the publication of this book, which I thusly consider a collaboration with you.

This research was supported by Sébastien Descours, at the Sorbonne, and Vincent Dahirel, from the Centre for Research and Interdisciplinarity, both in Paris. They provided me with insights and expertise that greatly assisted the research, although they may not agree with all of the interpretations and conclusions of this essay.

Above all I thank all the "Bridge Builders" for sharing their pearls of wisdom with me during the course of this research. They are an eclectic group of brilliant individuals who share - beyond their impressive contributions to the betterment of our world - great vision and a profound generosity, that was most visible in the time they so graciously spared me along my journey. I also am thankful to those who opened their doors to me and welcomed me in for a night or several months even, and to the friends who took time from their busy lives to visit me along the way. They helped me feel at home when I was far from mine.

I thank my patient proof readers for corrections and comments that greatly improved the manuscript. Any errors still left are wholly to be considered my own. Finally, I could not have done any of this without my family and friends. I am immensely grateful and forever indebted to them. Their help and support, both intellectual and emotional, are the true reason you have been able to read these words.

TABLES OF CONTENTS